The Daily Telegraph

IN SEASON

A YEAR OF READERS' RECIPES

EDITED BY

XANTHE CLAY

SIMON & SCHUSTER
A VIACOM COMPANY

First published in Great Britain by Simon & Schuster UK Ltd, 2005
A Viacom Company

Simon & Schuster UK Ltd
Africa House
64-78 Kingsway
London
WC2B 6AH

2 4 6 8 10 9 7 5 3 1

Design: Eye For Design

Copy editor: Nicki Lampon
Proofreader: Adèle Linderholm
Indexer: Michelle Baker, Indexing Specialists (UK) Ltd
Illustrator: Brian Gough
Cover illustrator: Paul Catherall

A CIP catalogue record of this book is available from the British Library

ISBN 07432 5965 3

Printed in Great Britain

INTRODUCTION

This book is about real food. Food cooked not by professional cooks but by real people, people for whom cooking isn't about earning a living, but about lots of other things, such as pleasing themselves and their families, nourishing them, too, satisfying a creative urge, producing meals that provide a focus for homelife, whether it's in a studio flat or a family house – all that while also doing all the other things that have to be done each day.

Often there's another, unrecognised benefit: providing a sense of continuity from generation to generation. Just as stories are passed down in families, so are recipes. Cooking and eating dishes that your grandmother made, and perhaps her grandmother, too, is an important part of preserving family, and national, history – the history of home cooking.

These days we're so in the thrall of the celebrity chef – Gordon, Anthony, Rick and the rest – that it's easy to forget that real home cooking is a completely different skill from restaurant cooking. Primping and fussing, foams and powders, recipes with seventeen steps that rely on a whole orchestra of trained kitchen staff, just won't do in the domestic environment. The atmosphere isn't right. Not that home cooking is inferior: it's just different, and food, like music, works best made in the right surroundings. You can't play a symphony on the guitar in the sitting room, but there are countless fantastic pieces you can play, which are as rich and thrilling in their way as the fanciest piece of music. Similarly, home food might be simpler, but it's just as fabulous. And I'd rather have a properly made toad in the hole than an incompetently executed seven-course menu, any day.

Working on the Readers' Recipes column in *The Daily Telegraph* gives me a privileged window into home cooking in Britain and beyond. I love getting the letters, reading through all of them, testing them, and of course, eating them. Then comes the tough part – choosing the ones to publish. If only I had more space… I'm continually impressed by how much you care about food, about good ingredients, about seasonality. Thank you for sharing your passion with me.

SPRING: MID‑MARCH TO MID‑JUNE

March 21st is the official start of spring, and I begin
to get hopeful as soon as the trees' branches show
a delicate fuzz of green and a bunch of daffodils
costs less than a cup of tea. Easter time is family
time, cooking up cakes and roasts – the first
spring lamb perhaps. And once it's over the
weather's on the up, the days are getting longer,
and we have summer to look forward to…

It's a long wait. Spring comes late to the
greengrocers in Britain. The first sign is English
asparagus mid-April, then tiny baby turnips,
prettily flushed with mauve. Fruit takes even
longer, with imports still making up the bulk
until the strawberries come in, themselves
heralding the start of summer.

I get over my impatience by foraging for wild food.
This isn't just for country dwellers … delicate young
nettle tops flourish in city parks and gardens,
pungent wild garlic grows thickly on roadsides.
Otherwise it's back to the veg shop for spring
greens and pointy spring cabbage, robust enough
to survive the often-bitter March and April weather.
New potatoes too: there are lots of varieties now,
with subtly different flavours and textures, good
for salads. Salads in these chilly, wet months?
Yes, now, when it should be sunny but isn't, I turn
to warm salads to get me through – far from frugal affairs,
but with the crisp brightness of fresh salad leaves beneath –
my defiant stand against the rain.

1

AVOCADOS

The avocado pear has had a chequered history. The Aztecs endowed it with aphrodisiac powers, calling it *ahuacatl* or "testicle" for its shape. Spanish missionaries were forbidden to plant avocado trees for their lascivious connections. More recently, the avocado pear became the star of Seventies' dinner parties, only to be denounced as clichéd. Finally, and worst of all, it has been inextricably linked with yellow-green bathroom suites.

But the buttery smooth flesh and gently nutty flavour of the avocado pear has weathered all the storms (the early sailings to the Americas carried avocados, which the sailors spread on bread and called "midshipman's butter"). It's the perfect partner for seafood and citrus; the saltiness of one and the tang of the other pointing up its mild creaminess. The most popular variety is the Hass avocado, sometimes called an "alligator pear" for its rough dark green skin that turns black when ripe. Smooth-skinned avocados like the Fuerte or the small-stoned Pinkerton are available too, as well as little sausage-shaped, seedless "cocktail" avocados.

AVOCADO & BEETROOT GRATIN
Serves 2-4
Preparation time: 10 minutes
Cooking time: 5-10 minutes grilling

Avocado pears can be eaten warm, although you have to be
careful. Too much heat turns them slimy and flavourless, so quick
cooking under the grill is perfect. Here, blue cheese and beetroot
balance the rich creaminess in this brilliant, beautiful pink and
green gratin. Ready cooked, vacuum-packed beetroot is fine for
this, but check it has no vinegar in it. Eat this dish with a plainly
cooked piece of fish, or just with good bread and wine.

> 250 g (9 oz) beetroot, cooked
> 1 avocado
> 5 tsp double cream
> 100g (3½ oz) Dolcellate cheese
> lemon juice to serve (optional)

Slice the beetroot and avocado into a fireproof dish, with the
beetroot on the bottom. Drizzle over the cream and top with
thin slices of the cheese. Pop under a grill for 5-10 minutes
until the cheese is beginning to brown. A squeeze of lemon
juice is good on this.

June and Bob Dawson, Rugby, Warwickshire

AVOCADO CREAM
Serves 6
Preparation time: 10 minutes + 2 hours chilling

Wherever the avocado is grown it is eaten as a sweet dish, mixed with sugar and lemon or lime juice. In this version, a splash of port transforms the bland sweetness into a really lush pudding. Serve it in small quantities with crisp biscuits, and cream or mascarpone if you're feeling piggy.

>   3 ripe avocados, stoned, peeled, and diced
>   6 tbsp sugar
>   juice of 1 lemon or lime
>   2 tbsp port wine

Mix all the ingredients, except the port, together in a bowl and mash until the mixture is smooth. Add the port and refrigerate for at least 2 hours.

Anne de Saint Hubert, Portsmouth

- Among fruits, only olives have more fat than avocados, but both are high in monounsaturated fat, so relatively healthy. Avocados are also exceptionally high in protein and nutrients, including Avocados vital Omega-3 fatty acids, the same as those found in oily fish.
- Choose avocados that are heavy for their size and uniformly hard or soft with no especially soft patches. Shake them and reject any with stones that feel loose.
- Freeze pureed ripe avocado flesh, mixed with half a tablespoon of lemon juice per fruit and closely covered, for up to two months.
- Early season avocados are lower in oil, containing about 12% rather than the 20% of late season avocados. They'll be more watery, less creamy, and less nutty than later ones.

BANANAS

We British have taken this fruit to our hearts, even though
it's only been common in this country for the last hundred
years, since the introduction of refrigerated shipping. Bananas
are a neat package, which must, in part, explain their popularity.
The sustaining carbohydrate-rich flesh is kept fresh and clean
beneath the easy-peeling skin. No washing, no knives, no spoons:
perfect food on the go. But all this would be as nothing without
that subtle, sweet flavour and easy-going texture that make
bananas the stars of the fruit world.

Bananas are a good bet early in the year, at their best when
there's little other fruit in season. If you can, choose Fair Trade
bananas with their distinctive logo, and support small growers
devastated by the collapse in world prices.

Before the recipes, here's a quick banana idea. Put a whole
banana in the freezer. The next day the skin will have turned
black; peel it off, or cut the banana in half and eat the inside
using a teaspoon. It's the most fantastic instant ice cream,
perfect for dieters with a craving for a rich, creamy treat.

CURRIED BANANA SOUP

Serves 6
Preparation time: 20 minutes
Cooking time: 25 minutes simmering

Banana soup might sound bizarre, but in fact bananas make
very good savoury dishes. They are no sweeter than carrots or
parsnips, and the plantain, used as a vegetable in Africa and the
Caribbean, is just a large, starchy banana. This soup is supremely
delicious, creamy with a subtle, intriguing flavour. Serve it in
small quantities since it is rich, with croutons, or, better still,
sweet potato crisps.

    50 g (1³/₄ oz) butter
    1 onion, finely chopped
    1 clove garlic, finely chopped
    1 tbsp mild Madras curry powder
    110 g (4 oz) Basmati rice
    1.2 litres (2 pints) chicken stock
    250 ml (9 fl oz) single cream
    2 ripe bananas, peeled and cut into chunks
    juice of ¹/₂ lime
    salt
    coarsely ground black pepper

Melt the butter in a saucepan. Add the onion and garlic and cook
until transparent and soft, then stir in the curry powder and cook
for 2–3 minutes more. Add the rice and chicken stock and bring
to the boil. Simmer over a low heat for 25 minutes or until the
rice is soft. Leave to cool before pouring into a liquidiser. Add the
single cream and bananas and process until smooth. Return to
the pan, add the lime juice, and season sparingly with salt and
pepper. Gently reheat.

Fiona Lee, Gloucester

BANANA CHUTNEY
Preparation and cooking time: 1–1½ hours

So many chutneys lose the character of the original ingredient, but not this one. The result is a sticky yellow chutney, prettily flecked with red chilli, and with a good banana flavour.

     12 bananas, mashed
     110 g (4 oz) sultanas
     225 g (8 oz) sugar
     1 tbsp curry powder
     2 sticks cinnamon
     600 ml (1 pt) white wine vinegar
     1 tbsp salt
     2 large onions, chopped
     1 red chilli, chopped
     8 small cloves garlic, chopped

Place all the ingredients in a large pan (not an aluminium one) and bring to the boil. Reduce the heat and simmer. Stir the mixture often to prevent it from sticking. When the mixture is thick (you should be able to see the base of the pan for a second when a spoon is dragged through the chutney), spoon into sterilised jars and seal with vinegar-proof lids.

Rona Cowls, Penzance, Cornwall

PLANTAIN TOSTONES
Serves 4
Preparation and cooking time: 20 minutes

Plantains are giant bananas, either green or yellow and black,
but their flavour is less sweet and more starchy than ordinary
bananas. And although ripe, yellow specimens are edible raw,
all plantains are best cooked. Peeled and boiled, green plantains
make a rather stodgy alternative to potatoes, while yellow
plantains are excellent baked or shallow fried. These plantain
crisps, or tostones, make a good side dish to a Caribbean curry,
or eat them with drinks before a meal.

> 1 plantain
> oil for frying
> salt

Peel a plantain (a slightly under-ripe one if possible) and cut
it into slices about 3–4 mm (⅛ in) thick. Heat a deep-fat-fryer
or a deep pan, one-third full of oil, to 160°C (310°F). Deep-fry the
slices for 4–5 minutes until they are soft but still pale. Lift out,
shake off any surplus oil, and cool in a bowl of iced salted water
for about 30 minutes. Drain, then pat the slices dry with a paper
towel. Make a well-spaced single layer of slices on a sheet of
greaseproof paper. Cover them with another sheet and, using
a rolling pin and firm, even pressure, roll the slices out to
a thickness of about 2 mm (1/16 in). Reheat the oil to 190°C
(375°F) and fry the flattened slices for about 1–2 minutes,
until crisp and golden. Drain thoroughly using paper towels
and serve sprinkled with salt.

G. Vernon, Christchurch, Dorset

BANANA JAM
Makes 1.25 kg (3 lb)
Preparation and cooking time: about 1-1½ hours

Creamy, but with delicious little bits of banana, this preserve has a rich, honeyed flavour. The lemon juice adds a tang that steers it well clear of being cloying. It is yummy on bread or toast, but just as good used as a topping for ice cream, pancakes, or waffles.

> 600 ml (1 pint) apple juice
> juice of a lemon
> 225 g (8 oz) granulated or preserving sugar
> 1 kg (2 lb 4 oz) bananas, peeled and sliced

In a large pan heat the apple juice, lemon juice, and the sugar gently until the sugar is dissolved. Add the bananas and bring the mixture to the boil. Simmer, stirring well to prevent the mixture sticking. When it is thick, the consistency of soft set jam, pot it up into scrupulously clean jars, and seal.

Jennifer Giannoccaro, Westerham, Kent

- Red, pointed banana flowers, for sale in ethnic shops, can be cooked and eaten too.
- Bananas are a particularly good source of potassium.
- A study in India recently indicated that eating bananas can help reduce high blood pressure.
- Ripen green tomatoes or hard avocado pears in a bag with a banana: bananas give off ethylene gas, which speeds the ripening process.
- Fully ripe bananas with brown patches have the best flavour for cooking.
- Tiny, very sweet apple bananas and red bananas with orange flesh, available from some supermarkets, are both delicious.

EASTER BAKES

Let's hear it for home-baked Easter cakes and biscuits and breads:
I'm fed up with cheap, mass-produced chocolate eggs. On the
Continent they really go for it with tarts and pastries and
specially plaited breads: presumably the three strands of the plait
represent the Holy Trinity. Generally the loaves are flavoured with
raisins and spice. In Greece, red-painted whole raw eggs are
pressed into the dough before baking (they cook hard in the
oven).

Here in Britain, Easter biscuits are more traditional Pascal fare.
They used to be spiced with cassia, a cinnamon-like spice, but
it's hard to find nowadays. No matter, most people consider
cinnamon to have a better flavour. Ideally, the biscuits should
be cut out with a large round crinkle cutter, but they work just
as well cut into bunnies and chicks. Little ones can decorate
them with tubes of writing icing, but to me the prettiest biscuits
are brushed with egg white and dipped in saucers of glittering
granulated sugar coloured palest pink, green, or yellow with
a knife-tip of food colouring.

CHOCOLATE EASTER BREAD, GREEK STYLE
Makes 1 large loaf or 2 smaller ones
Preparation time: 25 minutes + 80 minutes rising time
Cooking time: 25 minutes

I'm not sure that this is strictly authentic, but it is very good. It's gorgeous bread for an Easter Sunday breakfast – festive without being too rich or sweet.

  1.25 kg (2 lb 12 oz) strong white bread flour
  110 g (4 oz) chopped-up plain chocolate (or use any
       chocolate, even a Mars bar)
  110 g (4 oz) chopped prunes
  2 tsp salt
  2 tsp caster sugar
  1 sachet fast action yeast
  560 ml (1 pint) water
  2 medium eggs, beaten
  3 tbsp brandy or whisky (optional)

  To decorate
  4 tbsp milk
  4 tbsp water
  2 tbsp caster sugar
  3 sugar-coated chocolate eggs

Mix 900 g (2 lb) of the flour and the rest of the dry ingredients in a large bowl. Add the water, eggs, and alcohol, and mix. Knead well for 10 minutes (or 3 minutes in a mixer with a dough hook), adding enough extra flour to make a very soft, but not too sticky, dough. Cover the dough with greased cling film and leave to rise for an hour, or until doubled in bulk. Divide the dough into three, and roll each piece into a long sausage shape. Plait together, tuck the ends under, and place on a greased swiss roll tin. (This makes one huge loaf, but I find it easier to make two smaller ones and cook them on a baking tray.) Leave the loaf to rise again while you preheat the oven to Gas Mark 6/200°C/400°F. Bake for 20 minutes, then turn over and bake for 5 minutes more or until the loaf sounds hollow when tapped on the bottom. Cool on a wire rack. While the loaf is cooling, make a glaze by warming together the milk, water, and sugar. Brush the glaze over the loaf and decorate with the chocolate eggs – plain or painted with food colouring.

Suzie Hudson, West Runton, Cromer, Norfolk   11

EASTER BISCUITS
Makes about 30
Preparation time: 20 minutes
Cooking time: 15 minutes

These are perfect to bake on Easter Saturday with the children – it might even take their minds off Sunday's chocolate fest!

 350 g (12 oz) plain flour
 1 level tsp baking powder
 1 level tsp mixed spice
 1 level tsp cinnamon (or a few drops of oil of cassia)
 175 g (6 oz) butter
 175 g (6 oz) caster sugar
 110 g (4 oz) currants
 2 eggs, beaten

Sift the flour, baking powder, and spices into a bowl and rub in the butter. Stir in the sugar and currants. Mix in the eggs to form a stiff dough. Knead lightly and roll out to the thickness of a pound coin. Cut into rounds and bake at Gas Mark 4 180°C/350°F for about 15 minutes or until just coloured. Cool on a wire rack.

Sarah Campion, Chelmsford

FENNEL

Florence fennel is the aristocrat to celery's peasant. Which is not to denigrate celery: I love peasant food. And fennel does have a similar structure – fleshy, fibrous stems overlapping to form a bulbous head. But fennel has a more refined flavour, with hints of aniseed, a delicate scent, and a frankly better, less watery texture. It has none of that coarse bitterness, that can be celery's failing. Even the full name, which distinguishes the vegetable from fennel seed, suggests palazzos and Grand Tours.

Like celery, though, fennel is good both raw in salads and cooked. In salads it has a good but unaggressive crunch and a flavour that works well with the sweetness of oranges, peppers, and the like. Cooking fennel softens it and mellows the flavour. It takes particularly well to roasting or frying, caramelising to a gorgeous savouriness.

FENNEL WITH MINT, BASIL AND PINE NUTS
Serves 3–4
Preparation and cooking time: 25 minutes

This vegetable dish is excellent on its own, or you could use it as a bed for a piece of grilled white fish.

    4 bulbs of fennel, sliced
    2 cloves garlic, chopped (optional)
    knob of butter
    1 tbsp olive oil
    a handful of pine nuts
    6 sprigs mint
    4 large basil leaves
    salt
    freshly ground black pepper

Heat the fennel, garlic, butter, and olive oil in a covered saucepan and allow to sweat until the fennel begins to soften and take on just the edge of a light golden colour. Meanwhile, lightly toast the pine nuts in a hot frying pan. Roughly chop two-thirds of the mint and tear three of the basil leaves. Stir the leaves into the fennel, adding salt and pepper to taste. Cook until any liquid has evaporated, then tip on to a flat dish. Chop the rest of the herbs and scatter them over the top, along with the toasted pine nuts.

Yvonne Antrobus, Eye, Suffolk

FENNEL, RED PEPPER AND ORANGE SALAD
Serves 4
Preparation and cooking time: 20 minutes

Eat this salad on its own, as a first course, to properly appreciate the stunning contrast of colours, textures, and flavours.

3 red peppers
3 thin-skinned very juicy oranges
juice of ½ lemon
1 large or 2 small fennel bulbs, chopped
1 tsp mustard (Dijon)
salt
freshly ground black pepper
a slug of good olive oil
a few pink peppercorns (optional)
fresh coriander leaves to serve

Roast the peppers in a hot oven or under a grill until blistered and blackened. Pop them into a plastic bag to cool, then strip off the skins, stems, and seeds, and cut the flesh into thin strips. Top and tail two of the oranges and cut them into fine slices – as long as the oranges are really thin skinned, you can keep the skin on. Squeeze the other orange and mix the orange and lemon juice together with the mustard, salt, and pepper. Beat in the oil gradually. Place the fennel and roasted pepper slices in a salad bowl and mix in half the dressing. Arrange the orange slices on top, and trickle over the rest of dressing. Grind over some more pepper – a few crushed pink peppercorns look pretty and also taste good. Decorate with coriander leaves and serve at room temperature, not cold from the fridge.

Sheila Bennett, Paris, France

15

FENNEL, SPINACH, AND PEANUT SALAD
Serves 6
Preparation time:

Don't be daunted by the long list of ingredients here: you can substitute other vegetables, or leave things out. Just plain sliced fennel is gorgeous in the sweet-salt-spicy dressing.

100g (3½ oz) roasted peanuts
1 large or 2 small heads of fennel, thinly sliced
200g (7 oz) baby spinach, washed and dried
1 small cucumber, finely chopped
1 small red onion, finely chopped
2 tomatoes, finely chopped (optional)
2 oranges (optional)

Dressing:
1 tbsp vegetable oil
1 tsp sesame seeds
1 tsp mustard seeds
1 tbsp lemon juice
1 tsp sugar
1 tsp ground cumin
1 tsp ground coriander
salt
freshly ground black pepper

Coarsely crush the peanuts with a pestle and mortar or a rolling pin and mix together with the other salad ingredients. If you're using the oranges, cut off the peel and pith, slice the flesh into thin rounds, and add to the salad. To make the dressing, heat the oil in a small pan, then add the sesame seeds. Cook until light golden brown, then add the mustard seeds and cook for a few seconds more. Pour into a bowl, and allow to cool. Whisk in the other ingredients and season with salt and pepper. Drizzle over the salad and eat straight away.

Mrs Pratibha Vasudev, Lytham St Anne's, Lancashire

BAKED FENNEL WITH PARMESAN AND BACON
Serves 2, or 4 as a side dish
Preparation time: 15 minutes
Cooking time: 20-25 minutes

Baking fennel gives it a whole new character – sweet and
caramelised on the outside, tender and buttery within. This
version is savoury using Parmesan cheese, a favourite Italian
combination. Vegetarians will find the dish is still very good
even without the bacon.

   2 large heads of fennel
   60 g (2 oz) butter
   3 tbsp freshly grated parmesan
   1 clove garlic, crushed
   2 rashers of smoked bacon, chopped

Preheat the oven to Gas Mark 4/180°C/350°F. Remove the outer
layers of the fennel if they are tough or damaged. Slice each head
into three, cutting from top to bottom. Bring a pan of water to
the boil, drop the fennel in, and simmer for two minutes. Melt
the butter in an ovenproof dish big enough to take the fennel
in a single layer. Turn the fennel slices in the butter and sprinkle
the cheese, garlic, and bacon over. Bake for 20–25 minutes
until browned and bubbling.

Mrs S Parnell, Birkenhead

● Keep the feathery tops of fennel to use as a herb
   and a garnish.
● Put outer layers of fennel that are too tough to eat in
   the stockpot – they're especially good in fish stock.
● Try adding a splash of Pernod to fennel soups and braises
   to bring out the aniseed flavour.

NETTLES

Tumbling in the nettle patch was a regular feature of my childhood, so eating those nasty rash-inducing weeds seems counter-intuitive if not frankly looney. But stinging nettles have been eaten for hundreds of years in dock pudding, nettle beer, and Scottish kail soup. They are a springtime food: summer nettles are too coarse. So, put on your Marigolds and make for the hedgerows, or you'll be missing out on a seasonal delicacy. Of course, no one's suggesting you eat nettle salad. But cooked, nettles wilt down like spinach and all trace of sting vanishes to give a sweetish, herby flavour: nettles are related to garden mint. Choose a patch away from busy roads where they won't have been sprayed with weed-killer. Put on rubber gloves and collect the top leaves only of young plants – ideally not more than a foot tall. Reject entirely any that are in flower: they are too old. Wash your haul thoroughly and strip away all the stalks, which are so fibrous they used to be used to make cloth. Now you're ready to cook.

NETTLE AND POTATO SOUP
Serves 2–4
Preparation and cooking time: 70 minutes

You can eat this as a chunky, peasanty, meal-in-a-bowl, or liquidise it to make an elegant delicate soup. Stir in a little butter or cream to enrich it.

about 500 g (1 lb) unprepared nettles
½ large onion, roughly chopped
1.2 litres (2 pints) vegetable or chicken stock
225 g (8 oz) new potatoes or waxy old ones
¼ tsp ground mace or a blade of whole mace
salt
freshly ground black pepper

Prepare the nettles as on p.18 and chop the leaves roughly. Put them into a pan of boiling water for 3 minutes and then drain. Sweat the chopped onion slowly almost until transparent. Add the stock and potatoes and simmer for 20 minutes. With a potato masher, gently mash the potatoes so that they are broken up into pieces but not completely mashed. Then add the chopped nettles and mace (or a grating of nutmeg). Simmer for another 15 minutes, then season. Serve as it is, or liquidise to a puree.

Karen Pollak, Watford, Hertfordshire

SALMON WITH NETTLES
Serves 2
Preparation time: 30 minutes

Use just the very tips of the nettles to make this beautiful green puree to accompany salmon. It's fabulous with buttery mashed potato flavoured with nutmeg.

    2 large handfuls of nettle tips
    1 small onion, chopped finely
    glug of olive oil
    juice of 1 lemon
    2 pieces of salmon
    salt
    freshly ground black pepper

Wash the nettles in plenty of water and drain well. Fry the onion in the olive oil until softened but not coloured. Add the nettles and half the lemon juice, and cook gently for about 4 minutes. Meanwhile, poach or grill the salmon. Puree the nettle mixture in a blender or food processor, and season. Divide the puree between two plates and top with a piece of salmon. Squeeze over the rest of the lemon before serving.

Priscilla Park Weir, Camberley, Surrey

Yarg, the Cornish cheese, is wrapped in nettle leaves to encourage the development of cheese-ripening bacteria. The sting in nettles is the result of formic acid, HCOOH.

NEW POTATOES

New potatoes are best when they are really fresh. Whether they're true newbies (the ones the trade call "earlies") or their sisters, the waxy salad varieties, spuds eaten the day they are dug are indescribably good. Those of us who don't have a vegetable patch can at least chose dirty, soil-covered potatoes over bags of squeaky-clean ones. Washing them is a pain, but you'll be rewarded with a far better flavour.

STICKY TOFFEE NEW POTATOES

Serves 3–6
Preparation time: 20 minutes
Cooking time: 30–40 minutes

Herby, garlicky, slightly caramelised new potatoes. These are
perfect with roast meat, and divinely moreish. Although there
should be enough for six, three of us have no trouble at all
polishing off the lot.

  1 kg (2 lb 2 oz) small new potatoes, washed
  3 tbsp olive oil
  8 garlic cloves, peeled (smoked works well)
  chilli sauce (optional)
  4 large sprigs fresh rosemary

Preheat the oven to Gas Mark 8/230°C/450°F. Cook the potatoes
in boiling, salted water for 12 minutes. Meanwhile, heat 2
tablespoonfuls of the oil in an oven dish. Drain the potatoes
well, and stir them in the warmed oil with the garlic cloves.
Take a potato masher and gently bash the oiled potatoes until
their surfaces crack, but they remain whole. Pour another
tablespoonful of oil over the surface of the potatoes and sprinkle
chilli sauce over them to taste. Tuck the rosemary in amongst
the spuds. Roast for 30–40 minutes in the upper half of the
oven until the potatoes and garlic brown and become
slightly sticky.

Dr Mick Jackson, Crowborough, East Sussex

FRENCH POTATO SALAD
Serves 6-8
Preparation time: 30 minutes + cooling time

The bread crust adds an interesting texture to this salad, as well
as thickening the dressing, and the stock subtly enriches the
flavour. It makes a good alternative to a mayonnaise-heavy
traditional potato salad.

900 g (2 lb) small new potatoes
1-2 garlic cloves, crushed
1 thin bread crust
1 heaped tsp French mustard
2 tbsp white wine vinegar
8 tbsp olive oil
110 ml (4 fl oz) chicken or vegetable stock, hot
salt
freshly ground black pepper
a handful of fresh herbs such as parsley, tarragon, chives, or
    chervil, chopped

Steam or boil the potatoes, then skin them. Rinse them briefly
under cold water and dry them in a tea towel. Cut them into
5 mm (¼ in) rounds. Spread the crushed garlic on to the cut side
of the bread crust, working it in well. Cut the crust into
matchstick-thin pieces. In a salad bowl, mix the mustard and
vinegar, then whisk in the oil. Toss in the bread matchsticks,
then tumble in the potato slices and turn everything quickly
to mix. Pour over the stock and mix again. Season with salt
and pepper and leave to cool. Mix in the chopped herbs
before serving.

Mary Tarry, Limerick

RHUBARB

There's precious little fruit around February, bar imported
exotics, so thank goodness for rhubarb. True, the elegant slender
stems of the crème de la crème, day-glo, pink champagne
rhubarb are over now. But the thicker, somewhat more acidic
outdoor rhubarb makes good eating too, especially if it's
homegrown. The thing to be careful with is the texture: it can
easily be slimy and fibrous, just too much like school dinners.
For this reason, avoid anything green, and look for recipes
where the rhubarb is chopped, pureed, or strained.

RHUBARB AND ORANGE JAM
Makes 1.75 kg (4 lb)
Preparation and cooking time: 50 minutes + 15 minutes cooling

Mary Booth comes from a family of rhubarb producers and
passes on the wartime tip of adding a pinch of bicarbonate of
soda to the rhubarb to reduce the amount of sugar needed. She
also sends this great recipe for a full-flavoured, orange-scented
jam. It makes a good marmalade alternative at breakfast but is
splendid for tea or on a steamed pudding too. To test for the
setting point, turn off the heat and put a few drops of jam on to
a chilled saucer. After a few seconds, push the jam with your
finger. If you can see a wrinkled skin on your sample, then
the jam is ready.

　　6 oranges
　　1.35 kg (3 lb) rhubarb, cut into chunks
　　1.8 kg (4 lb) granulated sugar

Thinly peel the orange zest from the oranges in strips – a potato
peeler is ideal for this. Cut the zest into needle-thin strips.
Squeeze out the orange juice and put into a large pan along
with the rhubarb and orange zest. Cook gently until the rhubarb
has collapsed to a soft pulp. Add the sugar, stirring until
completely dissolved. Bring to the boil and boil for about
10 minutes until the setting point is reached. Allow to cool
for 15 minutes before potting into clean, hot jars.

Mary L Booth, Leadenham, Lincolnshire

RHUBARB AND DATE CAKE
Serves 6–8
Preparation time: 30 minutes
Cooking time: 90 minutes

Toffee-sweet dates can be cloying, but here the lemony tartness
of the rhubarb balances them perfectly. The cake is moist, light,
and moreish with a crumbly brown crust, good to eat for
pudding with clotted cream and more poached rhubarb.

    90 g (3 oz) butter
    170 g (6oz) self-raising flour
    110 g (4 oz) caster sugar
    225 g (8 oz) rhubarb, cut into 1 cm (½ in) dice
    110 g (4 oz) stoned dates, chopped
    1 large egg, beaten
    4 tbsp milk

Preheat the oven to Gas Mark 5/160°C/350°F. Grease and line
a 450 g (1 lb) loaf tin. Rub the butter into the flour, then stir
in the sugar, rhubarb, and dates. Mix in the egg and milk. Scrape
the rather thick mixture into the tin, hollowing out a shallow
trough along the middle. Bake for 90 minutes. Allow to stand
for 5 minutes before turning out of the tin to cool.

Mrs Edna Mardell, Dunmow, Essex

SPRING LAMB

Real outdoor-reared spring lamb, grass-fed (not pushed with
high protein feeds like earlier offerings), is at its best in May.
It isn't cheap, but the delicate milky flavour, cheesy oven
flavour, is exquisite. Strong spices and fancy techniques are
out of place since they risk reducing the meat to blandness.
Even plain roasting must be done gently or the dark caramelised
juices, so delicious with more robust meats, will overwhelm
the tender lamb inside.

SPRING LAMB WITH CRÈME FRAÎCHE
Serves 6
Preparation time: 90 minutes

This is the ideal treatment for a shoulder of spring lamb. Essentially a pale stew, the large pieces of meat make it look special, while the gentle acidity of lemon juice and crème fraîche counterpoint the sweet lambiness perfectly. It isn't overwhelmingly rich, but if you make the dish a day ahead you can refrigerate it and lift off any excess fat before reheating. Serve the lamb with spring vegetables, baby carrots, petits pois à la française, and Jersey Royal new potatoes of course.

1 shoulder of spring lamb
50 g (1½ oz) butter
2 small onions, finely chopped
1 tbsp plain flour
a bouquet garni*
salt
freshly ground black pepper
150 g (5 oz) crème fraîche
2 tbsp lemon juice
2 tbsp dry white wine
chervil or flat-leaf parsley, chopped

Trim as much fat as possible from the joint and cut the meat into 5 cm (2 in) dice. Heat the butter in a large pan and cook the onions until soft, but not brown, about 2–3 minutes. Add the meat and cook for another couple of minutes, turning regularly so it cooks on all sides but doesn't brown. Sprinkle over the flour and cook for another minute, stirring constantly. Add the bouquet garni and enough cold water to barely cover the meat. Season well, cover the pan, and simmer very gently for 50 minutes or until the meat is tender. When the meat is ready, scoop it out and put it in a warm serving dish. Stir the crème fraîche, lemon juice, and white wine into the remaining sauce. Raise the heat and bubble until the sauce is slightly thickened: it should be plentiful and the consistency of thin cream. Taste and adjust the seasoning. Strain the sauce over the meat and scatter over the chervil or parsley.

Annabelle Egginton, Sutton, Surrey

* A fresh bouquet garni is better than a ready-made dried one here. Just take a sprig each of parsley and thyme and nestle them in the hollow of a fingerlength of celery. Cover the herbs with a bayleaf and tie up the whole bundle with string.

SWEETBREADS

When spring is sprung, the lambs are in the fields, and
sweetbreads are here for their brief season – not calves'
sweetbreads, expensive and available for much of the year.
Lambs' sweetbreads are a spring delicacy, white morsels that look
and taste like the tenderest, creamiest little pieces of chicken. But
be warned – they shrink and coarsen as the weeks go by and the
lambs get bigger: adult sheep have no sweetbreads at all. So get in
there early and order them from your butcher. The first butcher
you ask may not be able to supply them, but persevere. Go to the
best butchers in town, the one who supplies the swankiest
restaurants, and they should be able to help.

So what are sweetbreads? Not testicles, whatever anyone says.
You can eat testicles, but they're pretty coarse fare. Sweetbreads,
by contrast, are delicate and impossible to take exception to.
Offal, yes, but a far cry from liver or kidneys. Sweetbreads are in
fact the young animal's thymus and pancreas glands, which are
generally referred to as the throat and stomach sweetbreads
respectively. They look much the same as each other, pale pink
slippery nuggets encased in a transparent membrane, but the
stomach sweetbreads are fatter and rounder. Some people prefer
these, but me, I'm glad for any sweetbreads I can get.

Preparing sweetbreads
This sounds a pain, but it's not hard and you can do it in advance.
The final cooking will be quick and easy too. First, soak the
sweetbreads in a big bowl of cold water to get rid of any streaks
of blood, which will spoil the ivory tones. Two hours is the
minimum, but overnight is better. You can also freeze the
sweetbreads at this point, in a plastic tub with enough water to
cover. Drain the sweetbreads and put in a large pan, covered
with fresh water. Bring to the boil and simmer for 5 minutes.
Drain, but keep the water, which is an excellent stock for soups.
Pull off any fat or tough membranes clinging to the sweetbreads,
but don't take off so much that the fragile flesh disintegrates.
Pile the breads on to a deep plate, and place another plate on
top, weighing it down with a couple of tins or suchlike – this
presses the sweetbreads to give them a firmer texture. Store
in the fridge for at least an hour and up to 24 hours.

29

SWEETBREADS WITH CREAM AND SHERRY

Serves 6

Preparing and cooking time: 30 minutes + up to 2 days to
prepare sweetbreads

Sweetbreads take well to a creamy sauce, and this one, boosted
with alcohol, is perfect. Don't leave out the fried bread, which
gives a good crunchy contrast.

> 1 kg (2 lb 4 oz) sweetbreads
> salt
> freshly ground black pepper
> plain flour
> 60 g (2 oz) butter
> 1 shallot, chopped
> 170 ml (6 fl oz) dry sherry or Madeira
> 280 ml (10 fl oz) whipping cream
> triangles of fried bread to serve

Prepare the sweetbreads as on p.29. Season the sweetbreads
with salt and pepper, and dust lightly with the flour. Melt the
butter in a large frying pan over a fairly high heat. Brown the
sweetbreads in the butter: do this in batches, transfering them
on to a warm serving plate. When all the sweetbreads are done,
use the same pan to cook the shallot until just golden brown.
Pour in the sherry and boil until reduced to half the quantity.
Pour in the cream, stir well, and cook until slightly thickened.
Season, and serve surrounded with the triangles of fried bread.

Martin Evans, Chester

WILD GARLIC

Drive or walk down a shady lane or past a wooded copse in April and there's a good chance the air will be filled with the unmistakable pong of garlic. Stop and admire the lush carpet of green leaves, similar to lily of the valley leaves, and the delicate umbels of white star-shaped flowers. This is wild garlic, traditionally known as ramsons – hence a host of place names, like Ramsbottom and Ramsey. The leaves taste powerfully garlicky raw; try them chopped in salads or as a garnish. Cooking them brings out the green, leek flavour. The flowers too have a strong flavour, concentrated in the pistils. Scattered over a plate of sliced tomatoes or a dish of risotto they look absurdly pretty. The roots can be used instead of garlic cloves. Joanna Harris in *Coastliners* writes of the French islanders cooking snails with wild garlic.

One of my favourite things to do with wild garlic is to use lots of leaves in a rustic soup with potatoes. Chop a big handful of leaves and stew them gently in butter. Boil a couple of peeled potatoes in some light stock, and add to the garlic pan. Whizz briefly with a hand blender or crush the potatoes with a masher, check the seasoning, and serve. If that sounds like too much trouble, then at least make some wild garlic butter. Chop 12–20 leaves roughly, then blend in the food processor with half a packet of butter – no need to add parsley. It freezes beautifully and makes wonderful garlic bread. Or, take a leg of lamb, spear it several times with a knife, push lumps of the butter into the holes, slather the whole thing with yet more of the vivid green butter, and roast it. Serve the lamb pink, with mashed potatoes to soak up the glorious buttery-garlicky juices.

CHICKEN WITH WILD GARLIC AND PARMESAN
Serves 2
Preparation and cooking time: 30 minutes

The garlic-wrapped chicken slices look beautiful here on the green-flecked rice, and any vegetarians at the table should be happy with the risotto alone, especially if you decorate it with a few garlic flowers.

> 2 boneless chicken breasts
> 60 g (2 oz) parmesan, cut into slivers
> salt
> freshly ground black pepper
> olive oil
> 12 wild garlic leaves

Preheat the oven to Gas Mark 6/200°C/400°F. Slice each of the chicken breasts two-thirds of the way through three or four times. Divide the parmesan slivers among the slits, pushing them well in. Season, drizzle with olive oil, then wrap each breast in about six wild garlic leaves. Bake for 20 minutes. When done, slice the chicken parcels. Serve with a simple risotto (with added chopped wild garlic leaves) and a green salad.

Peter de Stroumillo, Forest Row, East Sussex

SUMMER: MID–JUNE TO MID–SEPTEMBER

What's summer about? Strawberries of course, warm from the sun (nothing's more disappointing than a bowl of fridge-cold berries) with cream and a scattering of sugar. The best bit of all? The last scrapings of sweet, pink, fragrant cream, still gritty with sugar crystals… June on a spoon.

But there's more to summer than strawberries – the fragrance of elderflowers captured in cordial, the whiff of smoke from a barbecue. Summer supper parties are simple, with bowlfuls of simmered samphire to start with – exciting and new to those unfamiliar, a delicious treat to those in the know. Or fresh figs and proscuitto, or a simple salad of green beans. Then sardines – cooked on the barbecue perhaps – or salmon (organically farmed – if you knew what happened to the conventionally reared sort, believe me, you wouldn't want to eat it) and a salad spiked with leaves of lemony sorrel. Pudding would be those strawberries, or, later, melon and blackberries, with thick cream and lavender-scented sugar. Summertime and the living is easy…

AUBERGINES

To salt or not to salt, that's the aubergine question. We used to
do it to extract the bitter juices, but with modern varieties there's
no need to scatter the slices with salt and wait for acrid juices to
seep out before proceeding with a recipe. That being said, it's still
worth doing unless you're just going to bake them whole or grill
slices. Pre-salting reduces the amount of moisture in a dish and
firms up the texture of the vegetable. It also seems to limit the
oil soaked up when frying, that can otherwise be dyspepsia-
inducingly rich.

You may have seen a dazzling array of differently coloured and
shaped aubergines in markets abroad. Fat, skinny, pea-sized,
magenta, striped, or ivory white (hence the American "egg
plant"), they make our uniformly purple-black, comma-shaped
ones seem prosaic. But our aubergines make good eating,
especially in late summer when they are cheaper and plentiful.
And the exotically beautiful varieties can conceal bitterness, so
if you bring some home be sure to salt them before you cook.

How to salt (degorge) aubergines
Cut the aubergine in slices or chunks as directed by the recipe.
Put in a bowl and toss with 2 tbsp salt. Tip into a sieve or a
colander and place a plate on top. Put the whole lot in the sink
or in a deep dish to catch the drips, and put a weight (such as a
tin of beans) on the plate. Leave for about an hour, by which time
salty juices will have oozed out. Rinse the aubergine well, and dry
it in a tea towel before proceeding with the recipe.

Aubergine Dip

Serves 4
Preparation time: 10 minutes
Cooking time: 15-25 minutes grilling

This is a Lebanese take on aubergine caviar, that delicious creamy dip, good as part of a mezze or by itself with toast and bits of raw vegetables. Although it has a smooth texture and a rich, smoky-sesame flavour, it's fairly low in fat, so it won't leave you feeling weighed down.

    1 large aubergine
    2-3 tbsp tahini (sesame paste)
    juice of 1 lemon
    2 cloves garlic, chopped
    salt to taste
    olive oil to serve

Cook the aubergine, turning under a hot grill until the skin blackens and blisters and the flesh is soft, about 15-25 minutes. Scoop the flesh out of the skin and whizz it in a liquidiser with the tahini, lemon juice, garlic, and a pinch of salt. Taste the mixture, adding more salt or lemon juice as required. Pour into a dish and drizzle over a little olive oil.

Joyce Lambert, Wisbech, Cambridgeshire

AUBERGINES AND MUSHROOMS
Serves 2–3
Preparation and cooking time: 25 minutes + 1 hour to salt the aubergine

Good with simply cooked meat.

> 1 medium aubergine, sliced as thick as a pound coin
> salt
> 2 tbsp olive oil
> 175 g (6 oz) mushrooms, sliced
> 1 large garlic clove, crushed
> half a small tin of anchovies, chopped
> handful fresh oregano, chopped

Cut the aubergine slices in half if they are very large and salt them (see p.34). Heat the olive oil in a sauté pan and cook the rinsed aubergine slices until they are softening and very slightly brown. Add the sliced mushrooms and crushed garlic, and a little more oil if needed, cover the pan, and cook until the mushrooms are beginning to exude their juices. Stir in the anchovies, cover, and cook a few minutes longer. Stir in the chopped oregano. Taste and add salt if necessary, remembering that the aubergine will retain some salt and that anchovies are also salty.

Rosanagh Evans, Crockett, California, USA

Barbecues

Black Bean Chicken
Serves 3-6
Preparation time: 5 minutes + 2 hours marinating or overnight
Cooking time: 20 minutes

This brilliantly simple recipe uses chicken thighs, which have
a great flavour and don't dry out as easily as chicken breasts.
Here they cook to a shiny, dark-lacquered succulence, easy to eat
with your fingers, or, more conventionally, on a plate with salad.

   3 tbsp dark soya sauce (use a Japanese or low-salt variety)
   1 tbsp black bean sauce
   2 cloves garlic, crushed
   6 chicken thighs, skinned and boned

Mix the two sauces and the garlic. Turn the chicken thighs
in the mixture and marinate for at least 2 hours, or overnight
if possible. To cook, lay each piece of chicken flat on the
barbecue and cook for around 10 minutes on each side.

David Sherlock, Oxton, Wirral, Cheshire

SALMON WITH GARLIC AND TOMATO
Serves 6-9
Preparation time: 15 minutes + standing overnight
Cooking time: 15-20 minutes

Fish is a rare sight at British barbecues, which is a shame since
our oily native fish is especially good with a bit of smoky flavour:
think of kippers, smoked mackerel, and smoked salmon. This
recipe really calls for a barbecue with a lid, which turns the
apparatus into an oven-cum-hot smoker, although it's still worth
trying the dish on an open barbecue or even wrapped in foil in
a conventional oven. The basic recipe is open to adaptation: you
can add almost any herb or zesty flavouring to the tomato and
garlic mixture.

> 5 cloves garlic, finely chopped
> 3 tbsp parsley, finely chopped
> 3 marinated sun-dried tomatoes, finely chopped
> 1 tsp salt
> 3 tbsp olive oil
> 1-1.6 kg (2-3 lb) salmon fillet

Combine the garlic, parsley, tomatoes, salt, and oil in a jar. Leave
to stand overnight in refrigerator. To cook, place the salmon
on a rack (or a piece of greased foil), skin side down. Cut two
slits right along the length of the fillet, without piercing the skin.
Spread the garlic mixture over the fish, getting plenty into the
slits. Place the salmon, rack and all, on the barbecue grid. Close
the barbecue lid and cook for 15-20 minutes or until done.
Lift the rack off, with the salmon still on it, using tongs and
oven gloves. Eat in slices with salad or grilled vegetables.

Brigid Smyth, Leap, Co. Cork, Ireland

LEMON-BARBECUED BREAST OF LAMB
Serves 4-6
Preparation time: 15 minutes + 2 hours marinating or overnight
Cooking time: 15 minutes grilling

My only quibble with this gorgeous, lemony fragrant dish, with
its caramel spiced juices, is that it's really best left to marinate
overnight before cooking. In our climate, expecting the weather
to hold for this long seems frankly presumptuous. But this is
worth the risk, especially as, if the heavens open, you can always
cook the lamb on a griddle or even under the grill, in which case
it would be great with a pile of buttery mashed potatoes. Breast
of lamb is good value but fatty, and one of those boned, rolled
shoulders of lamb, unrolled, would do just as well here, and
would be a meatier option.

> 1 boned breast of lamb, excess fat trimmed
> 1 onion, sliced
> a few sprigs of rosemary
> 5 tbsp olive oil
> 1 tsp ground cumin
> 1 tsp ground coriander
> 1 tsp ground paprika
> 1 tsp cayenne pepper, or to taste
> juice and rind of 1 lemon
> 4 cloves garlic, crushed
> 1 tsp salt
> freshly ground black pepper

Cut the lamb into largish pieces, but no bigger than a half
postcard. Toss the onion, lamb, and rosemary together in a bowl.
Mix the oil, all the spices, lemon juice, lemon rind, and garlic
with the salt and plenty of black pepper. Pour this mixture
over the lamb, turning until the meat is well coated. Cover and
refrigerate for several hours or overnight. Barbecue fairly close
to the heat until the meat is golden, slightly charred, and still
pink in the middle.

George Marriot, Burgh le March, Lincolnshire

BARBECUED CORN WITH CINNAMON
Preparation time: 5-15 minutes
Cooking time: 5 minutes grilling

Vegetables used to be under-represented on the barbecue,
although the rise of "med veg" means that lots of us grill
peppers, aubergines, and courgettes alongside the meat. Try
this way of cooking sweetcorn to turn it into a deeply savoury,
finger-licking treat.

> corn on the cob
> butter, melted
> salt
> freshly ground black pepper
> cinnamon

Parboil your corn on the cob for about 10 minutes. (If your corn
is young and sweet, you can skip this precooking.) When cool,
cut the cob in half widthways, brush with melted butter, season
well with salt and pepper, and sprinkle with a generous dusting
of ground cinnamon. Grill the corn for about 5 minutes, or until
golden, turning regularly.

Gillian Royale, London

- If you worry about undercooking chicken or pork on the
  barbecue, stick to lamb or beef, where a pink inside is a
  positive bonus.
- Throw branches of rosemary or thyme on the charcoal to
  scent the smoke and flavour the food.
- Deseed and flatten out peppers to barbecue alongside slices
  of aubergine and baby leeks. Serve with a trickle of herb or
  chilli oil, a scattering of crumbled feta cheese, and bowls of
  chilled hummus and tzatziki.
- Thickly sliced, parboiled potatoes, turned in olive oil, chopped
  rosemary, and salt, cook beautifully on the barbecue.
- Roll out bread dough very thinly and cook it on the barbecue
  for homemade flatbread.

BASIL

"Baasiil!"

Just thinking about basil and I hear Sybil's voice, haranguing John Cleese in *Fawlty Towers*. It makes it hard to take basil seriously. But basil is very serious, the king of herbs: the name is from the Greek *basilikos*, or royal. Asian basil, *Ocimum sanctum*, or holy basil, has sacred status in India.

Ten years ago, before the Delia revolution, you'd be hard pushed to find fresh basil, or fresh herbs generally, for sale. Hard to believe now, isn't it? Last summer my local supermarket even had a little stand dedicated entirely to basil. My guess is that ten years from now we'll find it astonishing that we ever put up with those horrid plastic boxes containing a piffling few leaves. That might just about do for rosemary or bay, but when it comes to basil or coriander, or any of the other "soft" herbs, we want lots – Handfuls, armfuls – of the stuff, for pestos, salsas, and salads, and strewn generously over all summertime dishes.

Whatever you do, never cook basil. Warm it through, yes, but getting it too hot for too long will ruin it. That is why bottled pesto, sterilized to give it a long shelf life, tastes musty and bitter. Not a patch on fresh pesto, regardless of whether you make it yourself or buy it from an Italian deli.

Thankfully, some supermarkets are selling decent bundles of basil now, at a price. You'll probably get a better deal at a greengrocer, particularly one that supplies local restaurants. Ask for bunches, even if they aren't on display, since they may be stored out back. Cheapest and often freshest of all will be the ethnic shops: if there's a good one in your area it's a fantastic resource.

BASIL OIL
Preparation time: 10 minutes

Pesto isn't just delicious, it's a great way of preserving a bunch of basil before it starts to go black and slimy – which can happen frighteningly soon after you buy it. More versatile, though, is deep-green basil oil. It will keep for weeks in the fridge, ready to be stirred into soups and drizzled over salads, distinctively sweet-aniseed pungent. Yum.

    basil
    olive oil

Strip the leaves from a bunch of basil. If you have enough – a good handful – you can chop them finely in a food processor with a little olive oil. Smaller amounts can be pulverized with a little oil in a pestle and mortar – which is harder work but gives the best flavour of all. Either way, stir in enough oil to give a loose dropping consistency, and store in a small jar in the fridge.

Billie Fleming, Hailsham

COUSCOUS SALAD WITH BASIL AND RED PEPPERS
Serves 4
Preparation time: 30 minutes + cooling time

You could use basil oil (see p.42) in this lemony, smoky salad.
I do like the leafy quality which lots of fresh basil gives, though.
The salad is open to variation – olives or those semi-dried
"sunblush" tomatoes would be good additions – but stick to
punchy flavours. Eat it with grilled or barbecued chicken or fish.

> 4 tbsp extra virgin olive oil
> 400 ml (14 fl oz) boiling water
> 250 g (9 oz) couscous
> juice of ½ large lemon
> 2 red peppers
> salt
> freshly ground black pepper
> a good handful of fresh basil

Place 1 tbsp oil and the water in a medium saucepan. Bring back
to the boil, add the couscous, and stir briefly with a fork. Cover
the pan with a lid, turn off the heat, and leave the couscous for
5 minutes to swell up. Meanwhile, cut the peppers into quarters,
deseed, and grill them skin side up until the skin is blackened.
Allow them to cool, then strip off the skin, and slice the flesh
into strips. Mix the rest of the oil with the lemon juice, and
season with salt and pepper. Mix this dressing into the couscous
while it's still warm. Leave to cool before adding the peppers
and roughly chopped, or torn, basil. Check the seasoning: it
may need a squeeze more lemon juice. Serve at room, not
fridge, temperature.

Sandra Speak, Dursley, Gloucestershire

BASIL BLOODY MARY
Makes 1.1 litres (2 pints)
Preparation time: 10 minutes + chilling time

Basil is said to have a calming effect, which makes it the perfect thing to add to that morning-after soother, the Bloody Mary. This good spicy mix will last a few days in the fridge without the basil and vodka, so you can whip it up in an afternoon ready for brunch the next day. Should you be contemplating detox rather than hair of the dog, then, without the vodka, it's a delicious Virgin Mary too.

> 1 litre (1³/₄ pints) tomato juice
> 100 ml (3½ fl oz) lemon juice
> 2 tbsp horseradish (creamed or sauce)
> 1 tbsp Worcestershire sauce
> tabasco
> vodka
> a big bunch of basil

In a large pan, mix the tomato juice, lemon juice, horseradish, Worcestershire sauce, and a decent slug of tabasco – taste to get the heat right for you. Bring gently to a simmering point and cook for 5 minutes. Allow to cool and then refrigerate. To serve, fill tumblers with ice and add a shot of vodka to each. Chop the basil fairly finely, stir into the Bloody Mary mix, and fill up the glasses. A whole basil leaf looks pretty floating on top.

Sophie Denby, London

- A pot of basil on the windowsill repels flies. Always pinch out the leaves at the top to encourage bushy growth.
- If you have a choice, opt for basil from sunny climes like Italy: it's fuller flavoured than greenhouse-grown plants.
- The classic pesto, pesto genovese, should be made from Genovese basil and Ligurian oil.
- Packing basil leaves in layers of sea salt makes a basil-flavoured salt for cooking and salads.
- Reject any basil that looks limp or has black patches.
- The most fragrant basil is the tiny-leaved dwarf basil, *Ocimum minimum*; look out for cinnamon, lemon, and purple basil too.
- Dried basil bears no relation to fresh, so don't use it as a substitute.

Bilberries

You'll have to take to the hills for bilberries since you won't find them in the shops but will see them growing wild on high ground, especially in the north and west of the UK. For centuries, locals in the know have scoured the moors for bilberries, not only for their rich flavour but also for their inky dye and medicinal qualities.

From the start of August to the end of September the low-lying shrubs with dark green myrtle-like leaves are laden with the dusky little berries. Mine come from the Derbyshire Peaks, where they are abundant, but Cheshire, Cumbria, and many other areas have rich pickings. The name varies from place to place: bleaberry, wimberry, hurtleberry, and, in France, myrtille.

Although bilberries resemble small, cultivated blueberries, they are a different species. Blueberries are a yellowish-green inside, with a mild herby flavour and a starchy texture, while bilberries are dark throughout with a distinctive wine-y taste. They make excellent jam, and a bilberry pie is one of the best British pies you can find. To make one, fill a pie dish with bilberries, or a mixture of bilberries and grated Bramley apples. Mix in four tablespoons of caster sugar to each teacup of fruit. Top with sweet shortcrust pastry and bake for 20 minutes at Gas Mark 6 200°C/400°F. Serve the pie warm or cold, with lots of cream.

BILBERRY GIN
Makes 1 bottle
Preparation time: up to 4 months

This recipe comes from my father-in-law, a veteran bilberry
picker. He uses a bilberry scrabbler, which he was given years
ago by a Scandinavian colleague. A dustpan-shaped implement
with a metal comb to pull through the bush, it makes gathering
fast and simple, although it enrages us plodding handpickers.
There's no wastage though: Colin gets double value from his
crop. First he makes a delicious liqueur with gin or vodka, then
he uses the alcohol-soaked fruit to make a boozy version of
the pie described (above).

> gin or vodka
> bilberries
> caster sugar

Take a half full bottle of gin (or vodka, or a mixture) and fill the
bottle up with clean juicy bilberries. Add 2 tablespoons caster
sugar. Cork and shake well. Shake weekly for a month, then taste
the mixture and add a little more sugar if necessary. Continue
with the weekly shaking for another 2–3 months. Strain the gin,
keeping the fruit to use in a pie.

Colin Leach, Sheffield

- Eyesight in particular is said to be improved by bilberries:
  pilots in World War II reported improved night vision after
  eating bilberry jam.
- When picking bilberries, do remember, as with all wild foods,
  to only gather some of what is available, leaving some for the
  local fauna, and some to allow the plants to regenerate.

BLACKCURRANTS

Blackcurrants are not rated as highly as redcurrants by chefs, perhaps because they don't make such a sparkling, jewel-like garnish. But their minty, rich flavour is extraordinarily good, and as if that wasn't enough, they are power-packed too: six blackcurrants have more vitamin C than a lemon!

BLACKCURRANT SYLLABUB

Serves 6
Preparation and cooking time: 25 minutes + optional
    chilling time

I find a plain syllabub a bit too rich for comfort, nothing
but cream, booze, and lemon. But this blackcurrant version
is sublimely delicious, like a creamy, fruity mousse given edge
and complexity by the sherry. Eat it by itself or with some thin,
crisp biscuits.

    225 g (8 oz) blackcurrants
    grated rind and juice of a lemon
    4 tbsp sherry
    280 ml (10 fl oz) double cream
    90 g (3 oz) caster sugar

Simmer the blackcurrants, lemon juice, and lemon rind together
for 5 minutes. Pass through a fine sieve and allow the resulting
purée to cool. Stir in the sherry. Put the cream, sugar, and half
the fruit purée in a large bowl and whisk with an electric beater
until thickened. Still beating, gradually add the rest of the purée.
When the mixture is as thick as softly whipped cream, spoon
it into glasses. Eat straight away or chill for a stiffer syllabub.

Nicola Tranter, Bradford on Avon, Wiltshire

CRÈME DE CASSIS
Makes about 2 litres (1¾ pints)
Preparation time: steeping time of at least 4 months

I can't think of a better way of preserving the powerful wine-like
flavour of blackcurrants than in blackcurrant liqueur, or crème
de cassis. It is gorgeous mixed with white wine to make a classic
Kir, but it's also good poured over strawberries or used in a sauce
for game. The blackcurrant leaves add a subtly spicy and very
authentic flavour.

>   1.1 kg (2.5 lb) blackcurrants
>   20 very small blackcurrant leaves
>   2 litres (1¾ pints) spirit such as gin, vodka, or eau de vie
>   675 g (1¾ lb) granulated sugar
>   140 ml (5 fl oz) water

Wash the blackcurrants, discarding the stalks. Allow them to
dry thoroughly, then put them into a large glass jar and add the
blackcurrant leaves. Pour over the spirit, which should cover the
fruit completely. Leave to steep for 4–5 months or longer; it can
only get better. When the time comes to make the liqueur, strain
the contents of the jar (keeping the alcohol), and remove the
leaves. Whizz the blackcurrants in a food processor and strain
the resulting mush through muslin or filter paper. Mix the mush
with the purple alcohol. Dissolve the sugar in the water over
a low heat, then simmer gently for 5 minutes to make a thick
syrup. Cool. Pour slowly into the blackcurrant mixture, stirring
continuously. Taste and stop adding syrup when the liqueur
seems sweet enough. Pour into bottles and seal. You can drink
this straight away, but it will improve with time.

Judy Pennick, St Bees, Cumbria

BLACKCURRANT CAKE
Preparation time: 15 minutes
Cooking time: 45–50 minutes

This cake is simplicity itself, and a fantastic way of showcasing the fabulously intense flavour of blackcurrants. It deserves a fat splodge of thick cream - not crème fraîche please since the fruit provides plenty of acidity.

    60 g (2 oz) butter
    110 g (4 oz) plain flour
    110 g (4oz) caster sugar
    1 egg, beaten
    200 g (7 oz) blackcurrants

Preheat the oven to Gas Mark 4/180°C/350°F. Rub the butter into the flour and sugar until it's the consistency of breadcrumbs. Mix in the beaten egg. Stir in the fruit very gently so as not to break it: it's best to use your hands for this. The mixture will look rather dry, but don't worry; the end result is very moist. Turn into an 18 cm (7 in) round greased ovenproof dish made of glass or china - the acidity of the fruit might react with metal and taint the cake. Bake for 45–50 minutes. Turn out carefully and sprinkle with caster sugar. This is best eaten at room temperature.

Terry Guile, Steyning, West Sussex

- Blackcurrant leaves can be dried to make a cleansing tea. They also give a minty flavour when cooked with blackcurrants.
- Dried currants aren't currants at all, but the small Black Corinth grape.

Easy Ice Cream

Homemade ice cream is one of the nicest puddings of all, but it can be hard work to make. The problem with most ice cream mixtures is that they need regular beating to stop them forming large crystals and becoming coarse textured as they freeze. Without an ice cream maker to churn them, you'll have to hover by the freezer in order to whip out the mixture and beat it smooth every hour or so. Not everyone has an ice cream maker, and even for those that do it's always useful to have simple, no fuss ice cream recipes that can be made in large quantities. All these recipes, based on a mousse mixture, have enough air in them to freeze to velvety ice cream without any help. Just whip up the mixture and freeze it; that's it.

HOMEMADE ICE CREAM
Serves 4
Preparation time: 25 minutes + freezing time

This disarmingly simple basic recipe came from Mrs Sizer's friend, now in her eighties, and it certainly has that failsafe, stood-the-test-of time quality. The potentially cloying cream and sugar are cut with a splash of lemon juice, rather than the more usual flavouring of vanilla. In fact, until the last century, vanilla was a rare exotic and lemon was used instead in simple ices. This version is light and gorgeous by itself, or with soft fruit, and is a perfect base for other flavourings like coffee or ginger, or a "ripple" of homemade jam.

    3 eggs, separated
    110 g (4 oz) caster sugar
    280 ml (½ pint) double cream
    1 tbsp lemon juice

Beat the egg yolks until frothy and light. Whisk the egg whites until stiff, add half the sugar, and whisk until stiff again. Beat the cream until it forms soft peaks, then fold in the egg yolks, egg white mixture, the rest of the sugar, and the lemon juice. Turn into a container and freeze.

Angie Sizer, Minehead

CRANACHAN ICE CREAM

Serves 6–8
Preparation time: 20 minutes + freezing time

This is an ice cream interpretation of classic Cranachan, that divine Scottish confection of cream, whisky, raspberries, and oats. I know shortbread is an inauthentic substitute for oats, but it gives the right grainy crunch once frozen. The alcohol is crucial to the flavour, but it also stops all that cream freezing to a brick. If you don't have whisky liqueur, use ordinary whisky and add extra honey to taste.

> 840 ml (1½ pints) double cream, whipped to soft peaks
> 110 g (4 oz) caster sugar
> 6 tbsp whisky liqueur (like Drambuie or Glayva)
> 2 tbsp honey
> 140 g (5 oz) shortbread biscuits, crushed into crumbs and larger pieces
> 170 g (6 oz) raspberries

Whip the double cream and sugar together. Stir the whisky liqueur and honey into the cream, then fold in the shortbread and raspberries. Scrape into a 2 litre (3½ pint) container and freeze. Eat on its own or, even better, with a lightly sweetened purée of blackcurrants.

Frances Walshaw, Swanage, Dorset

HONEYCOMB ICE CREAM
Serves 6
Preparation time: 25 minutes + freezing time

This ice cream is fantastic, sweet and caramelly with crisp
Crunchie-bar type pieces in it. Don't be alarmed by the idea
of making "honeycomb" - it's easy, really it is.

> 5 tbsp granulated sugar
> 2 tbsp golden syrup
> 1 tsp bicarbonate of soda
> 600 ml (1 pint) whipping cream
> 1 small tin condensed milk

Start by making the honeycomb. Heat the sugar and syrup
in a heavy saucepan until the sugar melts. Then boil the mixture
for 2-3 minutes or until the caramel is a deep golden colour.
Stir in the bicarbonate of soda; the mixture will foam up.
Quickly pour it on to a greased baking sheet to cool. Next,
whisk the cream until thick, then whisk in the condensed milk.
Crush the honeycomb into small pieces and fold almost all of
it into the cream. Spoon the mixture into a serving dish or
freezer box, scatter over the remaining honeycomb, and cover
closely with clingfilm before freezing. Use within 10 days.

Doreen Woolf, London

ELDERFLOWERS

They may not smell like much on the bush, but infuse freshly picked elderflowers in syrup or milk and it's another story. A winey, muscat perfume and faintly lemony flavour develop – very English, very summery.

ELDERFLOWER MOUSSE
Serves 6
Preparation time: 1 hour + chilling

Creamy and delicately perfumed, this is summery and unusual
on its own, or eat it with raspberries or gooseberries.

    4 elderflower heads
    400 ml (14 fl oz) creamy milk
    4 eggs, separated
    125 g (4½ oz) caster sugar
    1 sachet powdered gelatine
    140 ml (5 fl oz) double cream

Put the elderflowers and milk in a lidded pan, bring slowly to
the boil, then turn off the heat. Cover and leave to infuse for
10 minutes. In a large bowl, whisk the egg yolks with 90 g (3 oz)
of the caster sugar until thick, pale, and creamy. Boil up the milk
again and strain it. Pour it on to the egg yolks in a slow stream,
whisking constantly. Place the bowl over a pan of simmering
water and stir until the custard is thick enough to coat the back
of a spoon. Put 4 tbsp of hot water into a small pan, sprinkle over
the gelatine, and leave for 5 minutes to swell before heating very
gently until the gelatine is completely dissolved. Pour the gelatine
into the hot custard and stir. Leave the mixture in the fridge to
cool and thicken to the consistency of softly whipped cream.
Whisk the egg whites into soft peaks, sprinkle the rest of the
caster sugar in, and whisk again until stiff. Fold into the cooled
custard. Allow it to set a little more, then whip the cream and
fold that in as well. Spoon the mousse into a rinsed-out 1.3 litre
(2½ pint) mould or serving bowl, cover, and leave it to set in
the fridge.

June Hare, Middle Rasen, Lincolnshire

ELDERFLOWER CORDIAL
Makes 1.7 litres (3 pints)
Preparation time: 30 minutes + up to five days infusing

Elderflower cordial is easy to make and much cheaper,
not to mention nicer, than the shop-bought variety.

In most recipes, citric acid acts as a preservative as well as adding
a sour zing, and I know many of you will have problems finding
it. Apparently it's used by drug addicts to make heroin more
soluble, so some chemists, such as Boots, won't stock it. You
should still be able to track it down at smaller chains and
independent chemists, or wine-making supply shops. Tartaric
acid is a possible substitute, although the acidity is a little
harsher. Failing that, just add extra lemon juice to taste and freeze
the cordial in ice cube trays rather than bottling it.

This recipe uses lots of flowers to get a really powerful flavour,
which I love.

> 2 kg (4 lb 8 oz) caster sugar
> 1.7 litres (3 pints) boiling water
> 40 elderflower heads
> 2 lemons, sliced
> 90 g (3 oz) citric acid

Dissolve the sugar in the water and mix all the ingredients in
a large bowl. Stir daily for up to five days: the lemon flavour gets
stronger, so I think three days is the optimum. Strain and bottle.
Store in a cold place and drink diluted with water.

Angela Bartlett, Shaftesbury, Dorset

ELDERFLOWER CHAMPAGNE
Makes about 6 75 cl bottles
Preparation time: 10 minutes + at least 2 weeks to mature

This dryish, lightly sparkling, and only mildly alcoholic drink is
a country favourite. Don't wash the flowers, just pick them
from unpolluted sites since the fermentation relies on naturally
present yeasts. This means it's a slightly risky recipe – there's
a cross-your-fingers' element as to whether it'll work or not.
But when it does, it's fabulous. Use screw-top bottles to bottle
the champagne, and screw on the tops loosely. Check the lids
from time to time and loosen them again to reduce the pressure
if necessary – otherwise they may explode. One reader suggested
using champagne bottles, which are heavier than wine bottles.
Your local restaurant or hotel may let you have empties.
Wine-making supply shops sell plastic champagne corks
and wires, which you should do up very tightly.

> about 24 elderflower heads (make sure they are newly
>   opened and dry)
> juice and rind of 2 lemons
> 450 g (1 lb) granulated sugar (add more if you like
>   a sweet drink)
> 4.5 litres (1 gallon) boiling water
> 2½ tbsp white wine vinegar

Put the elderflowers, lemon juice, lemon rinds, and sugar into
a gallon container (a bucket is fine). Pour over the just boiled
water and leave to cool. Then add the vinegar. Leave overnight
and bottle the next day. Wait for at least two weeks before
drinking – but it won't keep more than about six or eight weeks.

● Pick elderflowers that have newly opened and are dry.
● Put elderflowers in your bath for a summery smell.

Figs

Dusky, with a soft-as-skin exterior and a glistening flesh-pink
interior, and sugar-sweet, it's not surprising those sybaritic
ancients adored figs. They got to eat them at their best too,
freshly picked, still warm from the sun. Some lucky readers
did write to tell me of the loaded trees in their gardens, but
most of us are limited to imported Turkish figs, usually Mission
figs, deepest night-sky purple on the outside and sunset red
within. They make good eating, though, and are healthy too, with
plenty of fibre and ABC vitamins.

Fig Mousse

Serves 6
Preparation time: 35 minutes + 2-4 hours chilling

Subtle but not bland, there's no mistaking that nutty, figgy flavour
in this luxurious mousse. It is delicate, not firm textured, and too
fragile to make in a big bowl, so stick to individual ramekins.

    8 figs
    225 ml (8 fl oz) dry white wine
    4 egg whites
    125 g (4½ oz) caster sugar
    110 ml (4 fl oz) double cream

Poach the figs in the wine for about 15 minutes or until their
skins are soft. Mash the figs, chopping the skins into small pieces,
or liquidize them very briefly in a blender – you want to retain
some texture rather than produce a purée. Reduce the poaching
liquid until it is thick and syrupy, and allow it to cool. Whip the
egg whites until they form peaks, then add the sugar gradually,
beating well after each addition to keep the mixture stiff. Add a
quarter of the egg whites to the figs, and mix thoroughly before
folding in the remaining egg whites. Whip the cream until stiff,
carefully adding the reduced poaching liquid towards the end
while continuing to whip to retain thickness. Don't over beat
or it will curdle. Fold the cream into the figs and egg whites.
Pour into ramekins and chill for at least 2 hours, but don't
leave it more than 4 hours or it may split.

Michael Collins, Oxford

Fresh Fig Breakfast Bars
Makes 6–8
Preparation time: 10 minutes
Cooking time: 20 minutes

These are a sort of not-very-sweet, soft but chewy flapjack – plenty of cinnamon saves them from being too worthy. Each one delivers a good whack of slow-burning complex carbohydrate in the shape of cholesterol-busting oats, as well as milk and fruit. They may not be as good as a proper sit down meal, but if you've got to have breakfast on the go they sure beat those sugary, fat-laden, commercial breakfast bars.

> 225 g (8 oz) rolled oats
> 60 g (2 oz) dried skimmed milk powder
> 30–60 g (1–2 oz) caster or demerara sugar
> 2 plump ripe figs, cut up very small
> ½ tsp cinnamon powder

Mix all the ingredients together. It will look too dry at first, but the moisture from the figs will be enough to bind everything. Turn into a greased 20-cm (8-in) square baking tin and bake at Gas Mark 4/180°C/350°F for about 20 minutes, or until set but not browned. Cut into 6–8 pieces while still warm.

Pam Pointer, Salisbury, Wiltshire

FRENCH BEANS

French, dwarf, bobby, wax, fine, string, snap: the roll call of names for green beans is bewildering. Broadly, they either have a round pod (and are generally stringless) or a flat pod. Few are actually French: they originated in the Americas and now Kenya exports vast quantities, while we prefer to grow coarser-flavoured runner beans. But in the summer you can sometimes find skinny, delicious haricots verts, really from France and hardly fatter than a piece of string. Anyway, any green beans except runner will work in these recipes.

FRENCH BEANS WITH GARLIC, OLIVES, AND ALMONDS
Serves 2
Preparation and cooking time: 25 minutes

This is an explosive combination of crispy-fried ground almonds, olives, and garlic. You could serve it with plainly cooked fish! but it's excellent on its own – good enough to send my vegetarian sister into raptures.

150 g (5 oz) beans, topped and tailed
1 tbsp olive oil
1 tbsp butter
1 heaped tbsp ground almonds
½ tsp nigella seeds (optional)
1 heaped tbsp chopped parsley
1 tbsp black olives, pitted and roughly chopped
1 fat garlic clove, crushed
salt
freshly ground black pepper
lemon juice

Cook the beans in boiling water until just done. Drain. Heat the olive oil and butter in a frying pan over a medium heat. Add the almonds and nigella seeds, and stir until the almonds just begin to colour. Add the parsley, olives, garlic, beans, salt, and pepper. Cook over medium heat, stirring frequently, until the beans are heated through. Squeeze over a little lemon juice and serve immediately.

Susan St. Maur, Colby, Isle of Man

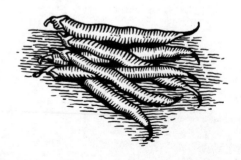

KARA DENIZ (BLACK SEA FRENCH BEANS)
Serves 6
Preparation time: 20 minutes

Tony Barley's grandmother lived in Giresun, Turkey, on the Black
Sea coast, hence this fragrantly spiced bean dish. Eat it with just
about anything (roast lamb springs to mind), and save the
leftovers to have cold.

    6 spring onions
    2 tsp fennel seeds
    3 tsp butter
    3 tsp olive oil
    2 tsp fresh root ginger, finely chopped
    500 g (1 lb 2 oz) French beans, topped, tailed, and halved
    salt
    1 tsp sesame seeds
    1 sprig of thyme
    freshly ground pepper

Discard most of the green leaves of the spring onions and slice
the rest very thinly. Grind the fennel seeds in a mortar. Heat the
butter and oil in a heavy pan. Add the ground fennel and the
ginger and fry gently for 2 minutes. Add the spring onions
and cook for another minute. Stir in the French beans. Add
4 tablespoonfuls of water, salt, the sesame seeds, and the thyme.
Cover and steam for 7–10 minutes until the beans are just
cooked and most of the liquid has steamed away. Serve hot
with a sprinkling of red or black pepper.

Tony Barley, Liverpool

- To stop green beans going khaki coloured and muddy tasting, precook them for 3 minutes in plenty of boiling water, drain, and run them under the cold tap until completely cold. To reheat, put a tablespoonful each of butter and water in a pan over a medium heat, and heat until melted. Add the beans and toss in the mixture until heated through.
- Choose plump, unwithered beans with a slight sheen to them.
- Yellow snap beans are plump and juicy and stay yellow, but beautiful purple beans turn green when cooked.

LEMONS

Lemons are a modern kitchen staple, indispensable, and endlessly useful. That sour kick transforms both sweet and savoury dishes, improving everything from strawberries to salmon. Lemon juice makes a good alternative to vinegar in summer salad dressings, giving a pleasantly fruity acidity, while the grated zest has flavour of its own, transforming plain biscuits and cakes with its pleasant citrus fragrance.

LEMON GERANIUM CORDIAL OR SORBET
Makes around 1 pint (600ml)
Preparation time: 35 minutes + freezing time for the sorbet

If you like elderflower cordial, then this recipe is for you.
Scented geranium cordial is far easier to make at home than
the elderflower version, and is, I think, just as delicious. More
properly called "pelargoniums", scented geraniums have been
used in cooking since the nineteenth century. Rose and lemon
scented geraniums are the most common, and either variety
works here. If you don't already have a plant, try a garden centre:
April and May are the best times to find them.

    170 g (6 oz) caster or granulated sugar
    15–20 lemon-scented geranium leaves
    juice of 2 large lemons
    2 egg whites, stiffly beaten (for the sorbet)

Bring 1 pint of water to the boil in a saucepan. Add the sugar and
stir until dissolved. Remove from the heat and add the geranium
leaves. Cover and leave for 20 minutes. Taste to check that the
flavour is strong enough. If necessary, reheat the liquid, add a few
more leaves, and leave to infuse once more. Strain the liquid and
add the lemon juice. This is the cordial. Poured into a sterilised
bottle and stored in the fridge, it will keep for 3 months. Dilute
with still or sparkling water to serve.

To make the sorbet, either follow the instructions on your ice
cream maker, or freeze the cordial in a plastic box. When almost
solid, beat it to break up the ice crystals (I do this in the food
processor). Fold the beaten egg whites into the mush and freeze
until firm. Like most sorbets, this is best eaten within a couple
of days.

Jeremy Dearling, King's Lynn, Norfolk

LEMON MILK JELLY
Serves 6–8
Preparation time: 30 minutes + overnight setting

Real homemade jelly is a treat, light years away from the
weirdly artificial sort you can buy in cubes or powders at the
supermarket. This one is both light and luscious, the perfect end
to a meal where fruit is not enough but anything else would be
too much. The eggs give the jelly a delicious, custardy texture and
flavour. As in many mousse recipes, the eggs are not cooked, so
use very fresh eggs from hens inoculated against salmonella
(i.e. with a Lion mark).

> 25 g (1 oz) sheet gelatine or 2 sachets of powdered gelatine
> 450 g (1 lb) granulated sugar
> 3 eggs, beaten
> 450 ml (16 fl oz) milk
> juice of 3 lemons

Put the gelatine sheets into cold water and leave to stand for
10 minutes. Drain the water off and squeeze out the excess.
Place in a bowl and pour over 225 ml (8 fl oz) of boiling water,
stirring to dissolve the gelatine. (If using powdered gelatine,
then pour the water into a bowl, sprinkle on the gelatine and
stir until completely dissolved.) Add the sugar and mix
thoroughly, until the sugar is more or less dissolved. Mix the
eggs with the milk and stir together with the gelatine mixture.
Last, add the lemon juice. Pour through a sieve into a jug, then
into a mould, and leave to set overnight in a larder or fridge.

Dennis Mason, Heckington, Lincolnshire

LEMON VODKA
Makes 1 bottle
Preparation time: around 5 days to mature

Unlike most alcohol recipes, which demand months of
maceration, this vodka is ready in only a few days. It's adaptable
too: instead of lemon, use chopped fresh ginger or a vanilla pod.
Drink the perfumed vodka with caviar, of course, or Scandinavian
style with pickled herring or crayfish, or on its own. Or make a
wildly fashionable scented martini with the vodka and the
geranium (or elderflower) cordial (see p.58).

    1 bottle vodka
    1 lemon, thinly peeled

Drop the lemon peel into the bottle of vodka. In a couple of
days the vodka will have turned yellow. Now taste the vodka
daily until the flavour is right: 5 days or so. Strain the vodka
into a clean bottle or just pull the lemon rind out with a pair
of tweezers. Drink ice cold from the freezer.

Jeremy Dearling, King's Lynn, Norfolk

- Choose lemons that are shiny and feel heavy for their size.
- Before using the rind in cooking, wash your lemons
  thoroughly to remove the preservative layer of wax.
- Store unwaxed lemons in the fridge.
- In the USA, look out for Meyer lemons – a mandarin-lemon
  cross with a sweeter, orange flesh.
- Lemons are usually picked while still green. They can take
  as much as a year to ripen on the tree.
- Menton on the French Riviera has a week-long Fête du
  Citron, staged every February. Around 130 tons of lemons
  and oranges are used to decorate the town.
- Sicilian lemons are especially fragrant and juicy.

LIMES

Limes are more than just a trendy alternative for lemons.
They have a distinctive smell and flavour, a whiff of pine,
a touch of bitterness. While lemons are a sub-tropical fruit,
limes are favoured in the tropics, and they go especially well
in hot-weather food, such as ceviche, Margaritas, mangoes....
Lime juice seems to carry more of the aromatic oils of the zest
than lemon juice, making the flavour rounder, more instantly
discernible. Blander tropical fruits, like papaya, would be nothing
without a squeeze of lime. But bear in mind that the juice is
more sour than lemon, so you may need to adjust the quantity
you use when substituting limes for lemons in recipes.

LIME AND CHILLI NOODLE SOUP
Serves 2
Preparation and cooking time: 30 minutes

Limes – pungent, sour, and fruity – are what you need to liven
up a jaded palate after rich food. This zingy soup is just right,
nourishing and light, like a detox in a bowl. Better still, it
squeezes the last bit of flavour and goodness out of the remains
of any poultry carcass and it's very adaptable. You could add
lightly cooked green beans, baby corn, and sugar snap peas. If
you have a stem of lemon grass, bash it with a rolling pin and
throw it in with the lime zest. Kaffir lime leaves added at the
same time give fragrance and a distinct oriental flavour: snatch
them up if you see them for sale and store them in the freezer.
Fancy something a little richer? Add a splosh of tinned coconut
milk. Oh yes, and if you can't face making your own stock, a
couple of cartons of ready-made stock will do just fine.

> 560 ml (1 pint) turkey, goose, or chicken stock (see p.203)
> juice and grated zest of a lime
> 1 green chilli, chopped
> 1 tbsp Thai fish sauce (optional)
> 1 tsp brown sugar
> 110 g (4 oz) rice noodles
> scraps from a poultry carcass
> salt
> 1 avocado, sliced
> a handful of coriander leaves

Put the stock in a large pan with the lime zest and bring to the
boil. Simmer for 1 minute. Stir in the lime juice, chilli, fish sauce,
and sugar. Add the noodles and simmer for a further minute, until
they are cooked. Stir in the scraps of cooked poultry and allow
to heat through. Season with a little salt, then serve in deep
bowls with slices of avocado and a scattering of coriander leaves.

Mark Brotherton, Newcastle

MACKEREL

We're all supposed to eat more oily fish – full of life-extending
omega–3 oils. Mackerel is a good choice for the faint-hearted,
less bony than herring, with more flesh than sardines, and
cheaper than salmon (even farmed salmon). Add to that a
delicious, almost chickeny taste, and you have the perfect fish.
Choose only really fresh fish, which will be bright eyed, red
gilled, and firm to the touch.

ALJOTTA

Serves 2–4

Preparation and cooking time: 40 minutes

Aljotta is a robust, Maltese fish soup or stew. Cooking the fish on the bone is a sure-fire way to a better texture and flavour, and filleting it before serving makes the dish easy to eat. Delicious with intense garlic and tomato flavours, it is also well-tempered: leftovers can be reheated.

    1 potato, cubed
    280 ml (½ pint) fish stock or water
    1 tbsp virgin olive oil
    4 cloves garlic, finely chopped or minced
    2 mackerel, gutted, topped, and tailed
    1 large onion, chopped
    2 heaped tbsp fresh thyme or marjoram (or 1 dessertspoon
        dried mixed herbs)
    400g tin chopped tomatoes
    2 large sun-dried tomatoes, finely chopped
    1 heaped dessertspoon concentrated tomato paste
    280 ml (½ pint) dry white wine
    2 mackerel, gutted, topped, and tailed
    a handful of parsley, finely chopped

Simmer the potato cubes in the fish stock for 10 minutes or so. Meanwhile, heat the oil and gently fry the garlic and onion in a large pan until softened. Stir in the herbs, tinned tomatoes, sun-dried tomatoes, and tomato paste. Add the fish stock, potato, and wine, and simmer for 10 minutes. Around 20 minutes before you wish to eat, add the mackerel and the parsley. Simmer until the mackerel is done: about 10 minutes. Lift out the fish carefully on to a plate and take the flesh from the bones, removing any skin that comes away easily in the process. Replace the pieces of fish in the pan and stir in gently. Serve the aljotta in deep plates with thick slices of crusty bread.

David Barker, Holmfirth, West Yorkshire

MACKEREL FILLETS WITH WHITE WINE, CREAM AND MUSTARD

Serves 2

Preparation and cooking time: 30 minutes

This is a cold mackerel dish, which sounds a bit odd. But mackerel is in the same family as tuna, and we don't think twice about eating cold tuna sandwiches. Poaching the fish makes it much less oily, and the light, creamy dressing is balanced by the acidity of the wine. I promise you, it's delicious: a perfect supper for a hot summer evening.

> 2 small mackerel, gutted
> ½ bottle white wine
> 1 onion, chopped
> 4 black peppercorns
> 1 celery stick or 1 carrot, chopped (optional)
> 1 tsp Dijon mustard
> 1 tbsp double cream
> a handful fresh parsley or chives, chopped

Poach the mackerel very gently in the white wine with the onion and black peppercorns. Add the celery and/or carrot to the cooking liquid if you like. Unless your pan is the perfect size for the fish, you may need to turn the mackerel after 5 minutes so that they cook evenly. After 10 minutes remove the fish and allow them to cool. Strain the liquid and pour half of it back into the rinsed-out pan. Boil until reduced by half, then mix in the mustard and allow to cool. Meanwhile, remove all the skin and bones from the fish. Mix the cream in with the mustard and reduced wine. Pour this sauce over the fish and sprinkle the dish with chopped parsley or chives. Eat with bread or a potato or rice salad.

Dr Tim Wharton, Lewes, East Sussex

Mangoes

Mangoes are the world's favourite fruit: more eaten every day
than apples or oranges or anything else. No wonder; mango
trees are prolific fruiters, and their fruit is soft and sweet
and delicious. Some are a tad fibrous, it's true, but the best
varieties avoid this. Mangoes can be green, or red, or yellow,
or a combination. Some types are as small as a plum, some
nearly a foot long. They grow in Africa, Asia, and South America,
with India as the biggest producer.

Every region has its favourite variety – although perhaps the
most esteemed is the Indian Alphonso, fragrant and juicy. It's
around in May, but in season for only a month. Then super-sweet
Pakstani mangoes, such as Chaunsa and Sindhri, are here until the
end of the summer. Look out also for the excellent Julie from the
West Indies, and the sticky-skinned Black mango, which is
actually yellow. Massage these small fruit in your hands, then bite
out a little hole in the pointed end. Suck the sweet juice out of
the skin – you'll get fibres stuck in your teeth, but the flavour is
sensational. If your mangoes come from the supermarket, you'll
probably be confined to varieties like Tommy Atkins or Keitt.
There's nothing wrong with these, but to keep prices down
they've been picked unripe and shipped over by sea, which
makes them dull flavoured. Worse still, they often turn rotten
without ever ripening to a proper juicy silkiness. Check out a
good African or Asian shop and find air-freighted mangoes, picked
ripe as little as 48 hours earlier. They may cost a little more, but
they should taste as good as the ones you ate on holiday.

Choose mangoes that are slightly yielding when squeezed, not
soft. Overripe mangoes are insipid. Use a sharp knife to cut the
mango "cheeks" from the large oval stone inside, and score the
flesh in a grid pattern, without cutting through the skin.

Now you can flip the "cheek" inside out to make a mango hedgehog, or simply scoop the chunks of flesh out with a large spoon. These will be very good eaten as they are, dressed with just a squeeze of lime. Or try 9-year-old Anna Jackson of Cambridge's recipe: simply whizz the flesh in a food processor with a scoop of vanilla ice cream. Squeeze in a little lime juice if you like, and eat as a fool or freeze until firm again. Vanilla, another tropical plant, is just right with the mango.

Don't forget how good the mango's slightly medicinal flavour can be with savoury as well as sweet food – I think mango makes a far better partner with parma ham than melon. Try cubes of mango with pan-fried foie gras, or pâté de fois gras – sublime.

Mango Salsa
Serves 4–6
Preparation time: 15 minutes

Try this as part of a Tex-Mex feast of tortillas, guacamole, refried beans, and sour cream.

> 2 ripe, medium mangoes (or 1 mango and 1 papaya)
> juice of 1 lime
> 1 small clove garlic, finely chopped
> 1 bunch coriander, chopped
> 1 mild onion, finely chopped
> salt

Chop the mango flesh into bite-sized pieces. Mix with the lime juice, garlic, and coriander, adding the onion to taste. Season with a little salt and leave to stand for a few minutes before eating.

Abigail Evans, London

Mango and Passion Fruit Sherbert
Serves 4
Preparation time: 20 minutes + freezing time

The dash of cream gives this ice the silky texture of fresh
mangoes, but you could leave it out and have a punchy-flavoured
sorbet instead.

> 6 passion fruit
> juice of ½ lemon
> 4 ripe mangoes
> 140 g (5 oz) caster sugar
> 60 ml (2 fl oz) double cream (optional)
> 1 egg white

Cut the passion fruit in half and scoop out the seeds and pulp.
Rub through a sieve to extract as much juice as possible. Add the
lemon juice to the remaining seeds and strain the juice through
the sieve again. Liquidise the juice with the flesh of the mangoes
and the sugar. Add the cream and egg white and liquidise again.
Freeze in an ice cream maker, or in a freezer box. If you use a
box, then cut the frozen ice into chunks and blitz to a smooth
consistency in the food processor. Then freeze again.

Carole Glen, Compton Bassett, Wiltshire

MELON

Supremely delicious, cooling, fragrant, and sweet yet never cloying. Melon may be the food of the gods, but naming them is the devil's own work. No one agrees. Take the Cantaloupe: Americans give the name to some musk, or "netted" melons – so called for the net of rough brown markings that seems to encase them. To us the Cantaloupe melon is a different species, although still sometimes netted. Green-fleshed Ogen and Galia melons are relatives, but the best Cantaloupe is orange fleshed, the most prized of all being the powerfully scented Charentais. Then there are winter melons – the vivid yellow, or yellow and green, smooth-skinned, ridged type, often shaped like a rugby ball. They include the Honeydew, with its delicate, palest-green flesh, pleasant enough but not a patch on the lush, headily flavoured Chanterais.

MELON AND TOMATO SOUP
Serves 6
Preparation time: 20 minutes + chilling

This is a chilled soup to bring out on the last warm days of summer. Creamy without being unduly rich, it's deeply melony, surprisingly filling, and delightfully fragrant.

> 2 medium ripe Cantaloupe melons, skins and seeds removed
> 500 g (1 lb 2 oz) tomatoes, skinned and deseeded
> 2 cucumbers, peeled and chopped
> grated zest of 1 orange
> 1 tbsp fresh mint, finely chopped (plus some for garnish)
> 200 g (7 oz) crème fraîche

In a food processor, blend the melon, tomatoes, and ¾ of the cucumber until smooth. Stir in the orange zest and mint, then whisk in the crème fraîche. Chill well, and serve sprinkled with the rest of the cucumber and mint leaves.

Wendy Davies, Wiltshire

MELON BRUTALE

Serves 4

Preparation time: 10 minutes + 20 minutes to stand

This unusual salsa-cum-salad is well worth trying with chargrilled meat or oriental food.

    400 g (12 oz) melon, cubed (a mixture of Galia
        and Honeydew)
    2 fresh figs, finely chopped
    1 onion, finely chopped
    1 red chilli, finely sliced
    1 tbsp fresh ginger, finely grated
    juice and finely grated rind of 1 lime
    1½ tbsp demerara sugar
    a good pinch of sea salt
    3 tbsp fresh mint leaves, finely chopped

Mix the melon cubes with the rest of the ingredients and let the mixture stand in a cool place for 20 minutes before serving. Serve it cold as an accompaniment to barbecued meat or fish and noodles with sesame oil.

Marie-Charlotte Jenkinson, Stockholm

- Choose melons with no splits or bruised patches; the best are scented, although some varieties have less natural scent than others.
- Only winter melons ripen well once picked, so a rock hard Cantaloupe is a lost cause. Press them at the non-stalk end and buy those that yield a little.
- Female melons are said to be better: they have a ring around the non-stalk end, like "the areola on a woman's breast" as *Larousse* delightfully describes it.

PINEAPPLES

It is said that if you can pull a leaf from the top of pineapple, this
is a sign that it is adequately ripe. However, it seems to me that
a leaf can be extracted just as well from an unripe pineapple,
so it's better to rely on the same rules that apply to everything
else. Does it smell ripe – strong, slightly astringent, and lemony?
Does it feel ripe – not rock hard, but with a little give? And does
it look ripe – even-coloured with no large greenish areas? The
ripeness issue is made more difficult by the fact that, according
to the growers and shippers, pineapples don't continue to ripen
once they are picked. But don't dismiss the rather elderly looking
pineapples with a greyish bloom on their surface. They can taste
the best. The interior may have the odd brown spot, but, as with
bananas, these seem to go with great sweetness and mellow
flavour. Perhaps this doesn't count as ripening, but as maturing,
what we used to call "bletting", as with dates and medlars.

For informal parties, I'm happy to slice the pineapple whole and let
people bite the flesh off the skin. For posher dos, or if my guests'
teeth are past their best, then it must be carefully peeled with
a sharp knife – a messy and laborious task. Look out for a pineapple
slicer/corer/peeler, a simple gadget that extracts a spiral of
pineapple flesh with minimum effort and very little waste. I've been
told it's unwieldy for left-handers, but for all other pineapple lovers
it's a worthwhile investment. Make sure you hold it over a bowl
to catch the juice, and make Piña Coladas to fill the empty shell,
with a pink umbrella, of course.

Fresh pineapple – and although tinned is OK for cooking, if you're
going to eat it uncooked it has to be fresh, unless you like being
transported back to school dinner fruit salad – is transformed by
a sprinkling of alcohol. Grand Marnier is good, but best of all is
Kirsch, a cherry-flavoured eau de vie, dry and with traces of bitter
almond, not to be confused with sticky cherry brandy.

PINEAPPLE AND BANANA SHERBET
Serves 6–8
Preparation time: 20 minutes + freezing time

Tip a measure of coconut rum over this tongue-tingling sherbet to complete the tropical fruit flavours.

    1 medium pineapple, chopped
    140 g (4 oz) caster sugar
    3 bananas, mashed
    juice of 1 large orange and 2 lemons
    2 egg whites

Whizz the pineapple and sugar together in a food processor, then add the bananas and lemon and orange juice. Whizz again to a purée. Pour into a shallow freezer box until nearly firm. Whisk the egg whites until stiff but not dry. Beat the half-frozen pineapple mixture until smooth, then stir into the egg whites little by little. Freeze again. Allow to soften slightly before serving.

Linda Herrick, Harrow

ROSEMARY

I used to have a huge rosemary bush growing by the front door,
an age-old sign that the woman's in control in the house. When a
daughter married, as she left her parents' house she would pick a
sprig from the bush and tuck it in her bouquet. When she arrived
at her new home, later in the day, she had the cutting to plant, by
the front door again of course. Now we've moved, you can
imagine how delighted my husband Richard is that there is
nowhere for my rosemary out front. But it flourishes year round
in the back garden, and I'm grateful for the pine-needle smell and
camphorous flavour, especially when other herbs are scarce.
Later in the year, as the new shoots grow, they have a greener,
fresher savour, adapting as well to summer cooking as the
woodier stalks do to winter dishes.

POTATO AND ROSEMARY GRATIN
Serves 4-6
Preparation time: 40 minutes
Cooking time: 90 minutes

This is a perfect Sunday lunch dish, great with just about any
roast meat, or with sauteed mushrooms for vegetarians.

> 3 tbsp olive oil
> 450 g (1 lb) onions, thinly sliced
> 900 g (2 lb) old potatoes, thinly sliced
> 2 garlic cloves, crushed
> 2 tbsp fresh rosemary, chopped
> salt
> freshly ground black pepper
> 280 ml (½ pint) single cream

Heat the oil in a lidded pan, add the onions, and cook covered
for about 30 minutes until softened and lightly coloured. Grease
a large gratin dish and layer the onions, potatoes, garlic, and
rosemary, seasoning as you go. Finish with a layer of potatoes
and pour over the cream. Cover with foil and bake for around
90 minutes at Gas Mark 5/190°C/375°F. The timing and
temperature can be varied according to what else you have
in the oven, but uncover it for the last 30 minutes so that it
can brown.

Nicola Tranter, Bradford on Avon, Wiltshire

ROSEMARY AND ALMOND BISCUITS
Makes 24
Preparation time: 20 minutes
Cooking time: 10 minutes

Rosemary works as well in sweet food as in savoury. Peta Groom
from Tunbridge Wells suggests adding rosemary to orange
marmalade (to eat with goose or duck) and to crab-apple jelly
(for lamb) – useful to remember when it's that time of year.
Or try these fragrant and buttery biscuits, divine with honey
or vanilla ice cream.

225 g (8 oz) plain flour
110 g (4 oz) caster sugar
60 g (2 oz) ground almonds
a good tbsp rosemary leaves, finely chopped
200 g (7 oz) soft butter
30 g (1 oz) chopped or flaked almonds

Preheat the oven to Gas Mark 5/190°C/375°F. Mix the flour,
sugar, ground almonds, and rosemary, then mix in the butter.
Put spoonfuls of the soft dough on to a greased baking sheet,
flattening each slightly and decorating with the chopped or
flaked almonds. Bake for 10 minutes until just coloured. Leave
for a couple of minutes before transferring to a wire rack to cool.

Cynthia Noble, West Malling, Kent

SAMPHIRE

You sometimes see samphire at the fishmongers – fleshy,
bright-green fronds piled up, masquerading as seaweed. The salty,
resinous flavour, with more than a whiff of the sea about it, has
a tang that reminds me of Thai fish sauce. In fact there are two,
unrelated, kinds of samphire. "True" samphire, or rock samphire,
Crithmum maritimum, grows on cliffs and in rocks and belongs
to the same family as fennel. It is said to be delicious, but it is
scarce. Marsh samphire, or glasswort (it was once used in the
glassmaking industry), grows along estuaries and on the salt
marshes. It is the kind you see for sale, and very excellent it is
too. June and July is the time to eat samphire, while it is still
young and tender. Although the season stretches into September,
it becomes tougher and more fibrous as the weeks go by.

Everyone agrees that samphire should be cooked simply. Store
it in a paper bag in the fridge (it will go slimy in a plastic one)
and pick it over before cooking. Very young samphire can be
eaten raw, but I generally boil it in plenty of water to reduce
the salt content. The timing depends on the age of the plant:
anything from 1 minute for baby fronds to 10 minutes for
tough old specimens. Serve it by itself as a starter, with just
a trickle of melted butter and a squeeze of lemon juice, and eat
it with your fingers, asparagus style, biting off the fibrous ends.
It's also good as a side dish, perhaps mixed with fresh peas and
young broad beans.

HOT "PICKLED" SAMPHIRE
Preparation and cooking time: 20 minutes + 48 hours soaking

Traditionally, samphire was pickled, and there's no doubt it
benefits from a bit of acidity. Here's a great recipe for an instant
hot pickle, that works with both marsh and rock varieties.
It is gently sour, making it delicious not just with fish but with
lamb too – which sounds strange until you remember laverbread,
another maritime vegetable, is the traditional accompaniment
for Welsh lamb.

> 2 good handfuls of samphire
> 4 tsp cider vinegar
> 1 tsp caster or granulated sugar
> 1 tbsp butter

Soak the samphire in cold water for 48 hours, changing the water
once. (For very young samphire, this won't be necessary.) Drain
the samphire and put in a pan. Cook until tender (no need to add
more water – just what is still clinging to the leaves is plenty).
Add the vinegar, sugar, and butter, and cook hard until the juices
caramelise slightly. Serve straight away with fish or lamb.

Rosemary Lloyd-Williams, Haslemere, Surrey

● When gathering samphire, follow the wild food rule:
  only pick when it's abundant and never take more than
  half of what's there.

SARDINES

Fresh sardines are summer fish, big and fat and juicy in July and August. Very large ones are called "pilchards" and can be caught off the Cornish coast and made into a classic stargazey pie. The smaller, not yet full-grown fish prefer the warmer seas of the Mediterranean, which is where most of the fresh (and tinned) sardines in our shops come from.

Two things put people off sardines: the bones and the smell. Apart from the obvious (open the windows or put the extractor on before you start cooking), buy only really fresh fish, bright-eyed, firm-fleshed, and red-gilled, and you should avoid a terrible pong. Or fire up the barbecue and get round the pungency problem altogether – sardines are wonderful outdoor food. Bones are easily dealt with. Cut the head and tail from each sardine, and gut them. Remove the backbones by opening the stomach and flattening the fish out on the board, skin side up. With a rolling pin, tap and roll down the backbone gently, holding on to the tail end. Turn the fish over; the bones should have loosened so that you can pull out the backbone and plenty of the attached bones. Trim off the thin, bony flap at the head end of the fish, along with any obvious remaining bones – you can't get every one, but the tiny ones left should be too small to cause problems.

HERB SARDINES
Serves 2
Preparation and cooking time: 30 minutes

These moist, herby sardines are delicious, with no tricky bones.

    4 tbsp olive oil
    8 tbsp fresh oregano, thyme, flat-leaf parsley, tarragon,
        basil, or what you will
    3 tbsp plain flour
    salt
    freshly ground black pepper
    6-8 fresh sardines

Remove the bones as described on p.90. Now arrange three flat
plates in a row. In the first pour the oil, in the second put half
the herbs, and in the third put the rest of the herbs, the flour, and
seasoning. Dip each sardine in oil, then in herbs, then in the herb
flour. Cook on a preheated barbecue, griddle, or frying pan until
slightly crisp – 2-3 minutes for each side. Eat with a watercress
and rocket salad, dressed with a vinaigrette made from one part
lemon juice to three parts olive oil.

Kate Edwards, Runcorn, Cheshire

Jardines Sardines

Serves 2

Preparation and cooking time: 20 minutes

This recipe came originally from a Portuguese chef at Jardines in Hong Kong. Lavender is very trendy at the moment, cropping up in cakes, compotes, and ice creams. It seems an unlikely flavouring for fish, but in fact the lemony-rosemary flavour marries beautifully with the robust sardine flesh.

> 2 fresh sardines, washed and gutted
> walnut oil
> lavender sprigs, leaves and/or flowers
> 3 tbsp whole-grain white wine mustard

Make two or three slashes on each side of the sardines. Brush them with the oil and push a piece of lavender into each cut. Grill the sardines under a preheated grill (or on a griddle) until crisp and firm, turning once. Warm the mustard, diluting it with wine or water if necessary, and serve as a sauce.

John Miles, Rugby, Warwickshire

SORREL

Sorrel might look like rather wrinkled spinach, but it's a very special leaf. The flavour is mouth-puckeringly sour, eye-opening lemony – just the thing to add zing to summer dishes. Getting hold of it can be tricky, however. Remember the early nineties, when rocket came not in fat bunches and huge cellophane pillow packs, but in measly little plastic envelopes in the herb section of the supermarket? Sorrel has the same affliction now. The few wilting leaves pressed in the packet are enough to add tang to a salad, but for sauces and soups we need handfuls of the stuff, not mean little pinches. My mother always had a patch of sorrel in the garden – which is one answer. It's not difficult to grow, although being low to the ground like spinach, the slugs may be a menace. Remember to plant French sorrel, *Rumex scutatus*, rather than the less good common sorrel, *Rumex acetosa*. For useless gardeners like me, it's a better bet to order a bag of sorrel from the greengrocer. Cut out any very coarse stems, then cook it gently in a little butter, and watch while it dissolves into a grey-green purée. You can freeze this for later, or use it straight away as the base for a delicious, gently tangy soup, or mix it with cream as a sublime sauce for fish.

BREAST OF LAMB WITH SORREL
Serves 2-3
Preparation time: 15 minutes
Cooking time: 35-45 minutes

Breast of lamb is an underused cut, somewhat fatty but tender
and full of lamb flavour, and gratifyingly economical. The acidity
of the sorrel cuts through the richness of the lamb beautifully.
If you can't get hold of any sorrel, it's still worth making with
spinach. Slice the skin and pith from half a lemon, and cut the
flesh into little pieces to scatter amongst the spinach leaves and
add the requisite lemony sourness, then roll up the lamb and
continue with the recipe as below.

> 1 boned breast of lamb
> a handful of sorrel, washed
> salt
> sprig of rosemary

Preheat the oven to Gas Mark 7/220°C/425°F. Trim off as much
fat as you can from the lamb: you won't be able to get all of it.
Lay the lamb skin-side down, and spread the sorrel leaves over it.
Roll it up, then tie it up with string three times along the length
of the roll: it should be firm but not tight. Rub the skin with salt
and put a sprig of rosemary on top. Bake for 35-45 minutes
until golden and crispy on the outside and tender in the middle.
Rest for 10 minutes before cutting into slices.

Margaret Gill, Arnside, Cumbria

SUMMER DRINKS

When it's too hot to cook, but you want to make something
special, homemade summer drinks are the answer. They have
a zest, a freshness you'll never get out of a bottle. Just the thing
for whiling away a hazy summer afternoon…

STILL LEMONADE
Makes 2.3 litres (4 pints)
Preparation time: 10 minutes + overnight

This is a perfect traditional lemonade that squeezes every drop
of flavour from the lemons. It's good made with limes too: just
use two limes for every one lemon.

    6 lemons
    12 tbsp caster or granulated sugar

Grate the zest from the lemons and put in a large heatproof jug
with the sugar. Squeeze the lemons and add the juice to the jug.
Pour over 2 litres (3½ pints) boiling water, and cover with a
plate. Leave to stand overnight, then strain through a fine sieve
or muslin and chill. This makes a strongish lemonade, so dilute
it a little to serve if necessary. It keeps up to a fortnight in
the fridge.

Muriel Richards, Calne, Wiltshire

LITTLE GREY RABBIT
Makes 1 large jug
Preparation time: 30 minutes + cooling

I don't know why this old recipe for a gooseberry-scented
spritzer is named after a character from a children's book,
but, however unlikely it sounds, do try it. The gooseberry syrup
tinges the long, cool drink pink and gives it a subtle scent.
Think of the gooseberry taste and smell of a good sauvignon
blanc. Sauvignon is an excellent choice of wine to use too,
although most dry whites, except overpowering New World
chardonnays, will do fine.

>   900 g (2 lb) gooseberries
>   caster sugar
>   1 bottle dry white wine, chilled
>   sparkling water, chilled
>   sprigs of mint or borage

Stew the gooseberries with a splash of water and sugar to taste –
gooseberries vary so much in sweetness, it's impossible to give
an exact amount. Aim for a pleasant, not too sweet, result. Strain
through a fine sieve or muslin to make a gooseberry syrup –
don't push the solids through. Cool, then pour 300 ml (10 fl oz)
of the syrup into a large chilled jug. Pour over the wine, and
top up with sparkling water. Slip in sprigs of mint or borage
and serve straight away.

Louisa Barrie, Daventry, Northamptonshire

Summer Cocktail
Makes 1 large jug
Preparation time: 10 minutes

Although this is a Pimm's style drink, it's much less sweet, with a fashionable bitter edge from the angostura.

    2 tsp angostura bitters
    150 ml (¼ pint) gin
    150 ml (¼ pint) red vermouth
    fresh mint
    cucumber
    1 apple, lemon, orange, or a handful of strawberries
    300 ml (½ pint) lemonade
    300 ml (½ pint) tonic water

Mix the bitters, gin, and vermouth, and put in a jug with the mint, strips of cucumber skin, and any or all of the fruit. Dilute with the lemonade and tonic and serve in large glasses with lots of ice and more fruit.

Dick Passmore, Cranleigh, Surrey

WATERMELON

A simple slice of watermelon, cool and refreshing as a sorbet, is hard to beat. You could gild the lily with a few drops of rose water or a drizzle of lavender syrup, but why do more? Great suggestions for eating plain chilled watermelon include handing round slices after the main course to refresh the palate and give the host time to get pudding on the table, or eating it as a snack with slivers of salty, feta-like Eastern European cheese.

Nonetheless, while I'd always eat the first few pieces of a watermelon "straight up", a whole melon is a lot to get through, so it's useful to have some recipes. Remember that watermelon works well in savoury as well as in sweet recipes, and the puréed flesh is a magnificent cocktail base. Or, come the end of the summer, try the heavenly combination of watermelon and blackberries.

Pickled Watermelon Rind
Makes 1.75 kg (4 lb)
Preparation and cooking time: 90 minutes + 24 hours soaking

Here's a recipe that appeals to the housewife in me. Stripped of the tough outer layer and cooked, watermelon rind is surprisingly good to eat, like cucumber or courgette. Try salting and boiling it as in the recipe below, then serving strips with melted butter as a side vegetable. Or follow the recipe through to make a slightly crunchy, sweet pickle to eat with cold meats or burgers.

1 kg (2 lb 4 oz) watermelon rind
60 g (2oz) salt
1 lemon, washed and thinly sliced
5 cm (2 in) piece of ginger, peeled and sliced
2 garlic cloves, peeled
1 stick cinnamon
1 kg (2 lb 4 oz) granulated sugar
600 ml (1 pint) white wine vinegar
1 tbsp chilli flakes

With a vegetable peeler, peel off the thin, dark-green layer of the rind. Cut the rest of the melon into small pieces and mix it with the salt and 1 litre (2 pints) of water. Leave to soak for 24 hours. Rinse the pieces in a sieve and boil them in water for 30 minutes. Rinse again. Put the lemon, ginger, garlic, cinnamon, sugar, vinegar, chilli, and 600 ml (1 pint) of water in a pan and bring to the boil. Boil for 20 minutes. Add the melon pieces and boil the mixture for about 30 minutes (or longer), until the pieces are transparent and soft. Put the pickle in clean hot jars and leave for at least 1–2 weeks before eating.

Helene Ott-Moller

WATERMELON, CUCUMBER AND MINT SALAD
Serves 4–6
Preparation time: 20 minutes

This minty, lemony salad is a great way to finish a
watermelon up, worth trying even if, like me, you're wary
of fruit in non-pudding situations.

> 1 kg (2 lb 4 oz) watermelon
> 8 cm (3 in) piece of cucumber
> 2–3 spring onions, sliced finely
> 4 sprigs of mint, chopped
> grated zest and juice of half a lemon
> salt
> freshly ground black pepper
> 5 tbsp olive oil

Peel the watermelon and slice it into thin triangles. Peel the
cucumber and cut it into six lengthways, then slice it thinly
crossways. Spread the melon and cucumber on a plate and
scatter over the spring onions and mint. Whisk the lemon
juice and zest with a fat pinch of salt and pepper, then whisk
in the olive oil little by little. Taste and adjust the seasoning –
you may want to add a little more oil if your lemon was a
large one. Drizzle the dressing over the salad and serve.

Jenny Freeman, Wimborne, Dorset

● If you're put off by the black seeds in dark-green-skinned
   watermelons, choose green and white striped "tiger"
   watermelons, which have only a few white seeds.

AUTUMN

AUTUMN: LATE SEPTEMBER TO LATE DECEMBER

By the time autumn comes, I'm ready for the
change in the air. There's a wistfulness for those
warmer days, to be sure, but excitement too:
it's time to crack on after the frivolity of the
summer, to make plans, do proper cooking,
fill the store cupboard. Early in the season the
big pans come out for preserving, to capture
the glut of the harvest. I'll be down to the
farmers' market too, to pick up the jams and
chutneys from the Women's Institute stall –
you can find outstanding goodies here, in a
different league from factory made offerings,
so there's no need to feel guilty.

Then the clocks change, and shopping after work
takes on new thrill: I don't think I've ever grown
out of the excitement at being out after dark.
There's the prospect of long dark evenings,
parties, meals by flattering, warm candlelight.
And for food, autumn is a rich time. Out with
suddenly wishy-washy-seeming salads, in with dark,
winey sauces, mellow slow-cooked dishes, warm
and sensuous berries, game, big flavours to go with
the vibrant autumn colours.

AUTUMN PRESERVES

Keats called autumn the "season of mists and mellow fruitfulness"
– and it's still true. In kitchens round the country, steam from
bubbling pans mists the windows and gently maturing jars of
chutney, pickles, and jams restock the cupboards. If you haven't
got preserving yet, satisfy your autumnal urges with these easy
but very special recipes.

How to test for setting
I test for setting by putting a plate in the freezer, then whipping
it out to drop a ½ teaspoonful of jam on it. Then it goes back in
the freezer for a couple of minutes to cool. If the jam has formed
a skin that wrinkles when pushed with a finger, it's reached
setting point.

Pumpkin and Orange Jam

Makes 1.25 kg (3 lb)
Preparation and cooking time: about 90 minutes

If you're doing the carved pumpkin thing at Halloween, then jam is a satisfyingly thrifty way of using the pumpkin up come All Saints' Day. The glowing, orange, chunky-textured jam has a strong citrus flavour, that makes it a good marmalade substitute if your stocks are running low, or try it dolloped on pancakes with cream.

> 1.35 kg (3 lb) pumpkin, peeled and diced
> grated rind and juice of 3 oranges and 1 lemon
> 1.35 kg (3 lb) granulated sugar

Boil the pumpkin until tender in the minimum quantity of water. Drain thoroughly and mash with a fork. Add the orange and lemon rind and juice. Bring everything to a simmering point, add the sugar and stir until dissolved. Boil for around 20 minutes or until thick, testing regularly for setting (see p.103). Once it starts getting near to ready, be sure to turn the heat off while you wait for the sample to cool. When it's done, pot up into hot, very clean jars.

Sylvia Kent, Billericay, Essex

PLUM, APRICOT AND RUM CONSERVE
Makes 1.25 kg (3lb)
Preparation and cooking time: about 2 hours

This plum conserve has a gorgeous smoky flavour from a good
slug of rum together with unsulphured apricots – lovely brown
toffee-like things you should be able to find at the health food
shop. Adding the plum kernels gives it an almondy taste, which
I love, but leave them out if you hate marzipan.

> 1.8 kg (4 lb) plums, ripe and juicy, but not over-ripe
> 280 ml (9½ fl oz) water
> 175 g (6 oz) unsulphured dried apricots, chopped
> 1.4 kg (3 lb) granulated or preserving sugar
> 4–5 tbsp dark rum

Cut the plums in half, take the stones out and put the stones,
with the scraps of flesh still clinging, into a small pan. Pour the
water over the stones and boil for 10 minutes. Strain, keeping
both the liquid and stones. Put the destoned plums and chopped
apricots in a large, heavy-based pan and pour over the strained
liquid from the boiled stones. Crack some of the stones and
remove the kernels. Set the kernels aside. Simmer the plums and
apricots over a low heat for about 10 minutes, until the fruit is
soft, stirring often to prevent burning. Remove the pan from the
heat and stir in the sugar until it's dissolved. Return to the heat,
bring back to the boil, and cook rapidly for about 15 minutes,
or until setting point is reached (see p.103). Take the pan off
the heat and add the plum kernels and rum. Leave to stand
for about 5 minutes, then stir well and pot up.

Jean McPhee, Corsham, Wiltshire

BLUEBERRIES

Blueberries seem very American somehow, snacked on by
bears and baked into blueberry pies. I'm sure they feature in
Laura Ingalls Willder's books of frontier life, growing rampantly
in the moist, acid soil of North American woodlands.

Our native "blueberry" is the bilberry, which grows wild
on moorland (see p.46). But to most of us, without the means
to forage for wild foods, blueberries are the dusky, plump,
thumbnail-sized cushions sold by the punnet at the greengrocer
or supermarket. Although many of them are from the USA or
Eastern Europe, I'm delighted to find blueberries are grown in
Britain now too. Look out for the Dorset crop; they are gorgeous
to eat raw – juicy and blandly sweet, with a subtle spiciness.

Cooking brings out the flavour of blueberries, especially if
you accentuate it with lemon, vanilla, and a little cinnamon or
cloves. They are great baked in cakes, exploding to make moist,
purple-black pockets and adding a sweet tangy flavour.
Try placing half your favourite plain cake mixture in a tin,
scattering over a handful of the dark berries, then dolloping
over the rest of the mixture. Sprinkle with demerara sugar
if you like a crunchy, sugary crust, then bake as usual.

LEMON-BLUEBERRY MUFFINS
Makes 10
Preparation time: 15 minutes
Cooking time: 20–25 minutes

A muffin nirvana, simply bursting with fruit.

225 g (8 oz) self-raising flour
150 g (5 oz) caster sugar
1 tsp bicarbonate of soda
$^{1}/_{2}$ tsp salt
pinch of ground cloves
300 g (11 oz) fresh blueberries
30 g (1 oz) butter
225 g (8 fl oz) plain low-fat yogurt
1 egg
1 tsp lemon juice
1 tsp vanilla
grated zest of a large lemon

Heat the oven to Gas Mark 5/190°C/375°F and grease 10 muffin
tins. Combine the dry ingredients in a large bowl, then stir in the
blueberries. Melt the butter in a second bowl and beat it together
with the wet ingredients and the lemon rind. Stir the wet
mixture into the dry until both are just mixed – don't worry
about any lumps. Divide the mixture among the muffin tins
and bake for 20–25 minutes. Cool to lukewarm before turning
out and eating.

Bev Laing, Middleton Stoney, Oxfordshire

BREAKFAST BLUEBERRIES
Serves 1
Preparation time: 2 minutes

This is a sort of easy version of the original overnight-soaked muesli – Bircher muesli. Soft and sweet, fruity and wholesome, it tastes like a treat despite being very healthy. If you remember, take the blueberries out of the fridge the night before – they taste far better at room temperature.

> porridge oats
> apple juice, chilled
> plain live yogurt
> blueberries

Put a couple of handfuls of porridge oats in a bowl. Pour over the apple juice, just enough to cover the oats. Add a dollop of yogurt (Greek yogurt is especially good) and top with a generous handful of blueberries. Stir lightly, to swirl the ingredients together. Eat straightaway, or leave to stand for a few minutes first to soften the oats.

Aileen Jennings, Cranbrook, Kent

BRAMLEY APPLES

Cooking apples, or codlins, are a particularly British thing.
They don't grow well in other climates, nor do other countries
appreciate that sharp flavour or the way they collapse to an airy
puree, or even the way they keep a fresh apple tang better than
sweet apples in cooked dishes.

UPSIDE-DOWN BRAMLEY CAKE
Serves 6
Preparation time: 30 minutes
Cooking time: 45–50 minutes

This is a great Sunday lunch pudding, more of a flan than a cake,
with lots of apples on a thin sponge rather than a pastry base.
I love the tartness of the fruit, sweetened only a little by the
jam, but you may want to put a bowl of soft brown sugar on
the table.

> 2 tbsp fruit jelly or sieved jam (bramble or blackcurrant
>   is ideal)
> 3 large Bramley apples, peeled, cored and thinly sliced
> 100 g (3½ oz) self-raising flour
> ½ tsp baking powder
> 90 g (3 oz) caster sugar
> ½ tsp mixed spice
> 60 g (2 oz) butter, softened
> 1 large egg, beaten

Preheat the oven to Gas Mark 4/180°C/350°F. Grease a non-stick,
20 cm (8 in) round cake tin and put a circle of baking parchment
in the bottom. Loosen the jelly or jam with a teaspoon of boiling
water and spread evenly over the parchment. Arrange the apples
in a layer of neat concentric circles on the jam, gradually layering
the rest of the apples on top. Sift the flour, baking powder, sugar,
and spice into a bowl, and mix the egg and butter in thoroughly.
Spread this mixture carefully over the apples. Bake for 45–50
minutes until darkly golden and firm to the touch. Cool in the
tin, turning out when still just warm or at room temperature.
Serve with whipped cream.

Eleanor Knowles, Lostwithiel, Cornwall

SPICY APPLE CHUTNEY
Makes about eight 450 g (1 lb) jars
Preparation time: 30 minutes
Cooking time: 1 hour

Bramleys, the most famous codlins, are marvellously heavy croppers. Kind friends drop round with boxes full of huge, flattish, irregular fruit, and by November each year I've had my fill of baked apples. There's only so many bowls of apple purée and Greek yoghurt a girl can eat, so it's recipes using large quantities of Bramleys that appeal right now. Try this chutney, which is almost pure apple, none of the usual raisins bulking it out. It's a lovely sweet-spicy mix, but give it a few weeks to mellow before eating.

    2.35 kg (5 lb) Bramley apples, peeled, cored, and
        roughly chopped
    450 g (1 lb) muscavado sugar
    900 g (2 lb) onions, chopped
    1.1l (2 pints) malt vinegar
    30 g (1 oz) black mustard seeds
    2.5 cm (1 in) cube of ginger, grated coarsely
    1 tsp cayenne pepper, or a finely chopped chilli pepper

Put all the ingredients into a preserving pan, or a big, heavy-bottomed saucepan. Bring steadily to the boil, stirring frequently. Turn down the heat, and simmer gently, cooking it down to a jam-like consistency. This will take up to an hour; stir regularly so it doesn't burn. When a wooden spoon drawn across the top of the chutney mixture leaves an indentation, the chutney is ready. Allow it to cool a little, then spoon it into jars and cover tightly.

Gail Donaldson, Abbeymead, Gloucestershire

BUTTERNUT SQUASH

Pumpkin gets all the attention at this time of year – which is
a shame. There are so many other squash out there. Butternut
squash is the best of all, with its deep, egg–yolk-yellow flesh
and sweetly nutty flavour. Cut into chunks, drizzled with oil,
and simply baked in a hot oven, it's the perfect accompaniment
to an autumn roast. Don't throw away the seeds: spread them
on a baking tray, sprinkle with salt, and cook them in the same
oven for 15 minutes or so. Eat them with drinks before lunch.

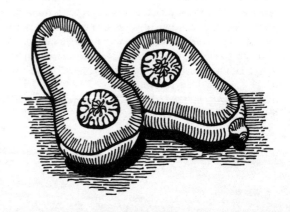

BUTTERNUT SQUASH AND HARISSA SOUP
Serves 4-6
Preparation time: 25 minutes
Cooking time: 80 minutes

A simple but intensely butternutty soup. The Morrocan spice
paste harissa adds zing and can be bought at most supermarkets.
Alternatively, use a little chopped red chilli and garlic, and a fat
pinch of ground cumin.

    1 large butternut squash
    salt
    freshly ground black pepper
    2 tbsp butter
    $^1/_2$ -1 tsp harissa paste (to taste)
    850 ml (1$^1/_2$ pints) chicken or vegetable stock
    1 tbsp crème fraîche

Heat the oven to Gas Mark 6/200°C/400°F. Cut the squash in half,
scrape out the seeds, season, and divide the butter and harissa
paste between each squash cavity, spreading some over the top
too. Place the squash in an ovenproof dish, cover tightly with foil,
and bake for about an hour. Once baked, scrape the flesh
and all the juices into a saucepan and add the stock.* Cover, and
simmer for 20 minutes or so. Tip the contents of the pan into
a liquidiser or food processor and whizz until completely
smooth. Return to the (rinsed-out) pan and heat gently. Add
the crème fraîche and stir gently to marble it through. If you
like, serve with shavings of parmesan, bits of crispy bacon,
or a few chopped chives.

Caroline Gilmartin, Bristol

* (In fact, if you're in a hurry, just chop the roasted squash, skin and all, into chunks
and put it in the pan with the stock. Sieve the soup after liquidising.)

BUTTERNUT SQUASH AND BLUE CHEESE RISOTTO
Serves 2–3
Preparation and cooking time: 35 minutes

Butternut squash is delicious enough to make a good standby
for visiting vegetarians, and everyone loves this lush, rich-tasting
amalgam of sweet squash and salty blue cheese.

    1 medium butternut squash
    4 tbsp olive oil
    2 cloves garlic, chopped
    ¹/₂ tsp chopped sage
    1 medium onion, chopped
    200 g (7 oz) risotto rice
    140 ml (5 fl oz) white wine
    850 ml (1¹/₂ pints) chicken or vegetable stock
    salt
    freshly ground black pepper
    225 g (8 oz) mild blue cheese, cut into small cubes

Preheat the oven to Gas Mark 6/200°C/400°F. Peel the squash
(a potato peeler works best for this) and chop the flesh into
2.5 cm (1 in) cubes, discarding the seeds. Put the squash cubes
in a roasting tray, drizzle with half the olive oil, scatter with the
garlic and sage, and toss together. Roast for about 20 minutes
until soft and just starting to colour. Meanwhile, heat the rest
of the oil in a pan, add the onion, and cook until soft, without
browning. Stir in the rice until coated with oil and turning
opaque. Tip in the wine and stir until it is absorbed. Add the
stock, a ladleful at a time, waiting until the last lot is mostly
absorbed before adding the next. Keep stirring! When the rice
is tender, but still with a bit of bite, add the squash and season
with salt and pepper. Cook for a couple of minutes, then take
off the heat and stir in the blue cheese. Serve immediately on
warmed plates.

Pamela Boston, West Malling, Kent

SPICED ROAST SQUASH
Serves 4
Preparation time: 15 minutes
Cooking time: 30 minutes

This gorgeous, spice-fragrant, caramelised squash dish was
developed by Gill and her cookery students at the Cumbria
Campus of the University of Central Lancashire. Eat it with
roast lamb or by itself as a supper dish.

   1 medium butternut squash
   6 slices streaky bacon, finely diced
   50 g (1½ oz) butter
   50 g (1½ oz) soft brown sugar
   ½ tsp cinnamon
   ½ tsp ground ginger
   ½ tsp ground cloves
   ⅛ tsp allspice
   ⅛ tsp ground cumin
   ½ tsp ground coriander
   salt
   freshly ground black pepper
   3 tsp made Coleman's mustard

Cut the squash in half, remove the seeds, and cut the squash
lengthways into wedges - around 8-10 pieces in total. Place
them in an ovenproof roasting dish, skin side down. Dry fry the
bacon with just a little of the butter to prevent it sticking to the
base of the pan. Then add the remaining butter and the brown
sugar. Add the spices, seasonings, and mustard, and pour over
the squash wedges. Roast at Gas Mark 6/200°C/400°F for
approximately 30 minutes until tender. Cover with foil for
the last 5-10 minutes if the squash is browning too much.

Gill Douglas, Penrith

DAMSONS

Little damsons, tiny blue-black plums hardly bigger than grapes,
are too tart to eat raw, and anyway the flesh-to-stone ratio is too
low to make them appealing eaten out of hand. But, stewed
with sugar in the barest minimum of water and sieved, they
have a vanilla, bitter-almond flavour with a winey intensity.
Use the purée as a sauce for game, to flavour mousses, or in
jam. Cooked whole they make wonderful pies and crumbles,
if a little heavy on the stones.

The season is short, so snap them up at the greengrocer or
gather them on country walks. If you do spot a tree full of fruit,
they may turn out to be round bullaces rather than drop-shaped
true damsons. They are interchangeable in recipes, but bullaces
are considered less good.

Even smaller than damsons are dusky black sloes, which are good
too but even tarter than their cousin the damson and need extra
sugar. Hold off until the first frosts before you pick them and the
flavour will be better and the skins less tough.

DAMSON ICE CREAM
Serves 6
Preparation and cooking time: 40 minutes + freezing time

This has such an intense, port-like flavour it's hard to believe
that it has no wine in it. Eat it in small quantities, perhaps with
a dollop of whipped cream.

> 450 g (1 lb) caster or granulated sugar
> 300 ml ($^1/_2$ pint) water
> 750 g (1 lb 10 oz) damsons
> 150–300 ml ($^1/_4$ –$^1/_2$ pint) lightly whipped cream

Dissolve the sugar in the water over a low heat, then bring to
the boil. Remove from the heat straightaway and leave the
syrup to cool. Heat the damsons gently in a pan until the juices
run and the fruit is soft. Rub the juice and fruit through a sieve,
getting as much of the fruit and skins through as possible. This
is a tedious job, but worth the effort; you should be left with
about 600 ml (1 pint) of purée. Whisk the cream, cooled purée,
and syrup together to produce a smooth cream. Freeze in an
ice cream maker or use a freezer-proof container. If the latter,
once it is frozen blitz it smooth in a food processor and return
it to the freezer.

Celia Jenkins, Llangollen, Wales

DAMSON KETCHUP
Makes 1.1 litres (2 pints)
Preparation time: 30 minutes
Cooking time: 85 minutes

This unusual damson ketchup is perfect for eating with cold meat. Sweet and unctuous, it makes a good present too.

> 900 g (2 lb) damsons
> 450 g (1 lb) demerara sugar
> a blade of mace
> 4 cloves
> 4 peppercorns
> $^{1}/_{2}$ tsp salt
> 300 ml (10 fl oz) vinegar (malt or wine)

Place all the ingredients except the vinegar in a pan. Heat gently until the juices run, then simmer for 15 minutes. Add the vinegar and continue simmering for an hour. Rub the mixture through a coarse sieve, return the sieved pulp to the pan and boil gently for 10 minutes, stirring well so it doesn't catch. Pot in wide-necked bottles and keep for at least two weeks.

Mr P. Donnellan, Walsall

DAMSON GIN
Makes 1 bottle
Preparation time: 30 minutes + at least 1 year to mature

This makes an excellent alternative to sloe gin, or use the same recipe for sloes, just doubling the quantity of sugar. Damson or sloe gin is best left a year at least to mature, although you could broach it at Christmas if the suspense is too much for you.

> 450 g (1 lb) damsons
> 90g (3 oz) sugar
> 75cl bottle of gin
> a preserving jar with a capacity of at least 1.25 litres
>   (2 pints)

Prick the damsons all over with a needle. Put them in the jar with the sugar and pour over the gin. Shake the jar every day for a month then leave until Christmas. Strain back into the gin bottle and use straightaway or, better still, keep until next Christmas.

Rachel Simhon, editor of Telegraph Weekend

- Damsons, like the fabric damask, owe their name to Damascus whence the little plums were first imported.
- Larger cultivated damsons are sometimes known as "damascenes", the name given to damsons imported from the Near East after the Crusades to distinguish them from the varieties of damsons already established in Europe.
- Damsons were originally grown to produce a purple dye as well as a food crop.

Garlic

Chicken Bearnaise
Serves 4
Preparation time: 20 minutes
Cooking time: 60–75 minutes + 10 minutes resting

I'm crazy for this dish. I guess it's "bearnaise" because it comes from the Bearn region of France: certainly it's nothing like the bearnaise sauce that goes with steak. Whatever. I've lost count of the number of times I've made it. Every time friends come for lunch, or we need a comforting, sustaining supper, this fits the bill. It's easy to make, doesn't need lots of fancy ingredients, and is plate-lickingly delicious. The meat is moist, and not especially garlicky since the garlic loses all its pungency to become a mild, melting, nutty garnish. Best of all, the chicken has a crisp golden skin (I've no time for chicken skin unless it's cracklingly crisp and salty), and it sits in its own pond of self-made gravy. No ordinary gravy this, but a rich, unctuous, flavoursome sauce that makes mashed potato compulsory. There's no need for anything more except a handful of rocket or curly endive on each plate. Hold the dressing and splash on more of that gravy.

> 1 medium-sized chicken
> half a lemon
> salt
> freshly ground black pepper
> 85g (3oz) butter
> 1 tbsp olive oil
> 225 g (8 oz) garlic cloves
> 140 ml (5 fl oz) chicken stock (I use a whole carton of fresh
>   stock so that there is lots of gravy)

Set the oven to Gas Mark 6/200°C/400°F. Rub the chicken all over with the lemon and season with salt and pepper. Heat the butter and oil in a large casserole dish and brown the chicken all over. Meanwhile, cook the garlic cloves in boiling water for one minute. Refresh in cold water and slip off the skins. Sprinkle over the browned chicken along with the stock. Cover and bake for 45 minutes, then remove the lid and baste the chicken. Return the uncovered casserole to the oven for 15–30 minutes until the bird is nicely browned and cooked through (pierce the thigh to check that the juices run clear). Remove the chicken from the pan and put it on a dish surrounded by the garlic cloves. Let it rest for 10 minutes in a warm place before carving. Whisk up the juices to make a rich gravy (spoon off some fat first if you like), pour some on each plate, and hand the rest around.

Peter Slaney, Modbury, South Devon

- Choose fat, hard heads of garlic and store them in a cool dry place, preferably not the kitchen (too warm) or the fridge (too damp).
- The cooler the climate it grows in, the milder the garlic is said to be.
- Purple garlic has a good flavour, but white garlic keeps better.
- When frying garlic never let it get beyond pale golden brown, or it will be bitter.
- Look out for huge heads of Elephant garlic. Actually part of the leek family, they are as large as a grapefruit and very mild.
- Fresh garlic, available in early autumn, has a moist green-white pliable skin and a tall stem, and is especially good.

GROUSE

The grouse season starts on the glorious twelfth of August,
but it's only at the end of September that prices drop from
stratospheric to more bearable levels. True, as the season goes
on, the grouse get older and a mite tougher. But while they might
not be as fat and tender as the August catch, they'll still have that
rich flavour of the heather moors. And although it's traditional to
serve one bird per person, the flavour is strong enough that with
plenty of sauce and good vegetables you can just about get away
with one between two.

GROUSE WITH BLACKBERRIES AND ROSEMARY SAUCE
Serves 2-4
Preparation and cooking time: 40 minutes

Trevor Maxfield's recipe for grouse with blackberries is simplicity
itself and makes the most delicious bird with copious amounts
of lush, deep-purple sauce. It's a great way of using the last
pippy blackberries, but it's just as successful with a bag of frozen
mixed summer berries. I often find savoury fruit sauces a bit
overwhelming, but not this: the herby, fruity acidity enriched
with grouse juices melds exquisitely with the gaminess of the
flesh. The original recipe is for oven-roasted bird, but late in the
season you're probably better off pot roasting, unless you're sure
your bird is young. I've given instructions overleaf.

2 young dressed grouse
150 g (5 oz) butter
300 g (11 oz) blackberries
1 tsp rosemary, chopped
4 rashers streaky bacon
salt
freshly ground black pepper

To roast, stuff the birds with the butter, blackberries, and
rosemary, and put them into a roasting pan with two rashers of
bacon over the breast of each bird. Roast in a preheated oven at
Gas Mark 5/190°C/375°F for 20 minutes. Tip the butter and berry
mixture out of the birds and pass it through a fine sieve, pressing
hard to get as much fruit pulp through as possible. Meanwhile,
keep the grouse covered in a warm place. Pour the sieved juices
into the roasting pan and reheat, stirring and scraping up the
browned bits sticking to the bottom. Season with salt and
pepper if necessary. Serve the birds whole, or cut in half along
the breastbone (use kitchen scissors), with the sauce and
accompanied by game chips (thinly sliced potatoes, fried until
crisp), red cabbage, or a celeriac gratin.

To pot roast the birds, heat a little butter in a heavy pan and
brown the birds all over. Remove them and splash half a cupful
of water into the hot pan, stirring and scraping up all the brown
juices. Stuff the birds and wrap in bacon as above. Put them in
a small casserole dish, along with the juices from the pan. Cover
and cook at Gas Mark 4/180°C/350°F for 30 minutes. Take the
dish out of the oven, and tip the berries and butter out of the
grouse into the casserole juices. Raise the oven temperature
to Gas Mark 7/220°C/425°F, pop the bacon-covered birds on
a roasting tray, and give them another 10 minutes in the oven
to brown them. Allow the grouse to rest for a further 10 minutes
out of the oven before serving. Sieve and season the berry
mixture and serve as a sauce, with accompaniments as above.

Trevor Maxfield, Cricklade, Wiltshire

ONIONS

Where would we be without onions? When I can't think
what to cook, I chop an onion and start it frying while I wait
for inspiration to strike. If I don't need it today, it will keep in
the fridge and save time tomorrow. That sweet-savoury taste
is the base note for countless dishes, while as star ingredient it
makes some of the best winter comfort food around. The thing
about onions is that they aren't fast food. No quick frying: they'll
just singe on the outside and remain hard and sulphurous within.
You need to lavish a bit of time on them to allow them to cook
properly, slowly soften, and, if necessary, caramelise. Not much
attention, though, so there's plenty of opportunity to get on
with other things in the kitchen.

UTE'S ONION CAKE
Serves 10 quantities can be halved
Preparation time: 30 minutes
Cooking time: 30 minutes

This German dish is a sort of cross between a pissaladière
(French onion pizza) and a quiche lorraine – filling and moreish
peasant food. The base is a scone mixture, but if you make your
own bread you could use some of the dough instead. It's good
hot, but leftovers can be eaten cold, or frozen for another day.

900 g (2 lb) Spanish onions
60 g (2 oz) bacon, cut into small pieces (optional)
60 g (2 oz) butter
up to 2 tbsp cumin seeds
3 eggs
110 ml (4 fl oz) sour cream
salt
freshly ground black pepper

Dough base:
110 g (4 oz) butter
450 g (1 lb) self-raising flour
pinch of salt
milk

Cook the onions and the bacon in the butter over a gentle heat
until soft. Meanwhile, make the dough by rubbing the butter into
the flour and salt, and adding enough milk to make a soft dough.
Knead lightly until smooth, then roll out onto baking sheets to
make two 22 cm (10 in) squares, pinching up the edges to form
a rim. Add the cumin seeds to the onions, cook for a moment,
then stir in the eggs, sour cream, and seasoning. Pile the mixture
on to the dough bases. Cook for 30 minutes at Gas Mark 4
180°C/350°F.

Bob and Hilary Pearce, Tadley, Hampshire

ONION AND SEVILLE ORANGE TART
Serves 4
Preparation and cooking time: 50 minutes

It'll take half an hour or more for the onions to cook to
a melting, sweet tenderness. But then you'll be able to make
this gorgeous tart – tangy and fragrant with Seville oranges.

> 675 g (1 lb 8 oz) onions, sliced thinly
> 70 g (2½ oz) butter
> juice and peel of 2 Seville oranges
> 2 sprigs fresh tarragon
> 30 g (1 oz) granulated sugar
> 170 ml (6 fl oz) white wine
> 20 cm (8 in) pastry flan case, baked blind

Heat the oven to Gas Mark 6/200°C/400°F. Soften the onions
in 55 g (2 oz) of the butter in a heavy-bottomed pan on a gentle
heat. Add the orange peel and tarragon and raise the heat to
medium to start caramelising the onions. Stir frequently. Melt
the remaining butter over a low heat and sprinkle over the sugar.
Cook gently until the sugar melts into the butter and turns a pale
toffee colour. Immediately add the orange juice, which will spit
and boil. Bubble until the toffee is dissolved in the juice to
make a syrupy liquid. Pour the wine into a shallow pan and boil
until reduced by two-thirds. When the onions have started to
caramelise, remove the orange peel and the tarragon, and add
the orange syrup and wine. Cook until thickened and the juices
are scant and the consistency of single cream. Fill the pastry
case with the onion mixture. Bake for 10 minutes, and allow
to cool before serving warm or cold.

Michael Collins, Oxford

ONIONS BAKED WITH ROSEMARY

Serves 4
Preparation time: 15 minutes
Cooking time: 30–50 minutes

These onions spread out to a pretty starflower shape in the
oven, and the rosemary and sugar mixture gives a slight crunch
as well as adding flavour to the soft, sweet, caramelised onion
petals. Eat them with lamb or game, or with salad leaves as
a vegetarian starter.

> 4 large onions
> 2 tbsp caster sugar
> 2 tbsp fresh rosemary, chopped
> a generous tablespoonful of butter
> salt
> freshly ground black pepper

Peel the onions, trim the root end leaving just the stump, and
slice downwards three times leaving the bottom intact. Place
the onions on a greased baking tray. They should splay out like
a water-lily. Mix the sugar and chopped rosemary with a little
of the butter, and carefully spoon the crumbly paste into the
onion cuts. Dab the rest of the butter on top, season, and bake
in the oven at Gas Mark 4/180°C/350°F for 30–50 minutes – they
should be well browned but not burnt. Serve with roast lamb
or game, or as a vegetarian starter.

Trevor Maxfield, Cricklade, Wiltshire

- Pearly-white onions are sweet and mild, as are Spanish onions,
  red onions, and the American Vidalia onions. All can be eaten
  raw or cooked.
- Ordinary brown onions, sometimes called "yellow" onions,
  should always be cooked.
- To make peeling large quantities of small onions easier, cover
  them with boiling water for 1 minute, then drain.

POMEGRANATES

The pomegranate features large in legend. Take poor Persephone. According to Greek myth, whilst imprisoned by Hades, she swallowed a mere six seeds of pomegranate and thereby condemned herself to six months in the underworld, and the rest of us to half a year of winter. Some experts identify the fateful "apple" of the Tree of Knowledge as the pomegranate – which cognates with the Persephone story. The fruit of doom all right, especially where women were concerned. Still, throughout Arabia and India, they love the pomegranate. And why not? Underneath the hard, leathery shell is a honeycomb of pink, jewel-like fruit. A bitter creamy-yellow membrane runs through and round; prise out the juicy morsels, each with a seed suspended within its glassy flesh. The flavour is elusive, sour-sweet, although the pip adds a bitter edge, so it's best not to chomp too hard on it. Make the most of the prettiness of pomegranates by sprinkling the rosy gems over salads and Middle Eastern dishes.

FAISINJAN
Serves 4
Preparation and cooking time: 1 hour

A faisinjan is a traditional Persian dish with a pomegranate and walnut sauce. Originally made with pheasant, now chicken or duck are generally used. This version uses lamb and is satisfyingly easy and exotic, the sweet nuttiness combining with the strong flavours of the meat to create a beguiling savouriness. It's even better made a day ahead.

    1 kg (2 lb 4 oz) boned lamb, cubed
    salt
    freshly ground black pepper
    butter for frying
    4 pomegranates
    2 onions, chopped finely
    225 g (8 oz) walnuts, ground finely
    juice of 1 lemon
    2 tbsp caster or granulated sugar
    560 ml (1 pint) lamb stock or water
    pinch of cinnamon
    pinch of nutmeg

Sprinkle the meat with seasoning and fry very slowly in the butter for about 30 minutes until almost cooked. Cut the pomegranates in half and pull out the pink seeds on to a piece of muslin or a tea towel. Keep a few in reserve. Wrap up the seeds and squeeze out the juice into a bowl. In a separate pan, cook the onions in butter until golden, then add the ground walnuts, mixing well. Pour in the pomegranate and lemon juices, and stir in the sugar. Add the lamb stock or water and the spices. Simmer for 15 minutes, stirring frequently. Add the meat to the sauce and continue simmering until the meat is very tender. Season to taste and serve with boiled rice, sprinkled with the reserved pink pomegranate "jewels".

Carol Wilson, Wirral

SLOES

Sloes are tiny, sour, large-pipped plums – a dusky-black colour, the fruit of blackthorn bushes. Gather them from the hedgerows while on a country walk. If you can't find any sloes, or only sparse amounts, take heart – next year you could be lucky. It seems that bumper crops are biennial. Or there may be another explanation. Although tradition has it that sloes will be bitter until after the first frost, canny sloe-lovers get in early and strip the bushes. It seems that a spell in the freezer replicates a frost, and since the skin splits as the fruit defrosts in alcohol, sloe gin makers don't need to prick each fruit first. There's no doubt this is briskly efficient and means the farmer's hedge trimmer doesn't get there first. Purists still prick their sloes with a silver needle. Experts also recommend a corn on the cob holder (safer) and rolling a nutmeg grater over a trayful of sloes (faster). After making sloe gin, a good idea is to take the same fruit and pour a bottle of cream sherry over it. Three months should be enough to give you a delicately flavoured, pink-tinted aperitif. I hear rumours of a gorgeous sloe gin ice cream too, made from the leftover fruit…

SLOE GIN
Makes 1 bottle
Preparation time: a year or more

Sloe gin is the most famous sloe recipe, a dark, port-flavoured liqueur of great richness. This is an amalgam of all the recipes sent in by *Telegraph* readers.

    450 g (1 lb) sloes
    225–450 g (8 oz–1 lb) caster or granulated sugar
    580 ml (1 pint) gin

Freeze the sloes or prick each all over with a needle. Feed them into a wide-mouthed bottle and use a funnel to pour over the sugar (how much will depend on how sweet you like your liqueur). Pour in the gin. Cover tightly and shake every day for 3 weeks, by which time the sugar should have dissolved. Leave for 2–3 months before straining, then bottle and keep for a year or more before drinking.

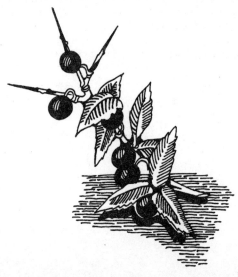

SLOE CHEESE
Makes
Preparation time: 30 minutes

This is a traditional English "cheese" – a thick fruit paste, similar to fruit jelly sweets. It was traditionally turned out of pots and served in slices with cheese, fruit, and nuts at the end of a meal. Try it with stilton for the Christmas cheeseboard.

> 2 kg (4 lb 8 oz) sloes
> 850 ml (1½ pints) water
> 280 ml (½ pint) port (or more water)
> 2 kg (4 lb 8 oz) granulated sugar
> glycerine

Rinse the sloes and put them in a pan with the water and port. Simmer gently until soft and mushy. Sieve the pulp and return it to the pan. Continue to cook gently until no liquid appears when you draw a spoon through the purée. Meanwhile, warm the sugar in a low oven. Tip the sugar into the pan and stir to dissolve it. Turn up the heat and cook, stirring constantly until the mixture is very thick. Brush some wide-mouthed pots (ramekins or teacups are fine) with glycerine, pour in the mixture and seal with cellophane circles.

Patricia McColm-Limberg, Camborne, Cornwall

SWEET POTATOES

The thing about sweet potatoes is that they must be orange
fleshed. Your greengrocer should be able to tell you if he has the
honeyed, aromatic, salmon-coloured flesh potatoes or the inferior
insipid, mealy white versions. In the supermarket, you will have
to make a tiny scratch in the terracotta skin and inspect what
lies beneath to be sure. Once you've got them home, you have
the makings of one of the simplest, nicest suppers, and healthy
to boot. Just bake the potatoes, one per person, in a hot oven for
about 40 minutes until soft. Split them open and add pepper
(and a dash of angostura bitters if you have it). Eat them out
of the skin with salad and perhaps a couple of rashers of lean
bacon. No butter: the flesh is already rich and spicy and creamy
in spades. One caveat, though – cook the sweet potatoes in
a dish, not straight on the oven shelf, since they leak sticky,
syrupy juices as they bake.

SWEET POTATO AND APPLE CARAMEL
Serves 8
Preparation time: 40 minutes
Cooking time: 1 hour + 2–3 minutes grilling

This sweet gratin recipe hails from Canada. Apples go fantastically well with sweet potatoes, diluting what can be a rather overpowering flavour. I fancy this might be intended to eat with meat – the North Americans are fond of very sugary vegetable dishes – but to me it's an unusual but remarkably good winter pudding.

700 g (1 lb 9 oz) sweet potatoes
60 g (2 oz) granulated sugar
1/2 tsp salt
1/4 tsp nutmeg
60 g (2 oz) butter
3 tart, crisp apples, peeled, cored, and sliced
4 tbsp hot water
140 g (5 oz) soft brown sugar

Preheat the oven to Gas Mark 4/180°C/350°F. Boil the potatoes for 20 minutes, then peel and slice them thinly. Mix the sugar, salt, and nutmeg, and blend in the butter with a fork. In a greased casserole dish layer one-third of the sweet potatoes and one-third of the sliced apples, and dot over one-third of the butter mix. Repeat the process twice more, and pour over the hot water. Cover with foil and bake for about an hour, until the apples are tender. Remove from the oven, sprinkle the brown sugar evenly over the top, and put under a hot grill for 23 minutes until the top is melted and bubbling, watching carefully that it doesn't burn. Serve with whipped cream.

Caroline Ambrose, Southport, Merseyside

SWEET POTATO AND TALEGGIO GRATIN

Serves 4-6
Preparation time: 20 minutes
Cooking time: 1 hour

Taleggio is a soft Italian cheese with a fruity flavour, but ripe
brie will do fine if you can't get it. The gratin is richly flavoured
and makes a good vegetarian meal by itself. However, the
sweet-savoury taste is irresistible with roast lamb, and perfect
for Sunday lunch.

> butter
> 225 g (8 oz) Taleggio (or brie), sliced
> 1 fat garlic clove, crushed
> 700 g (1 lb 9 oz) sweet potatoes, peeled and
>   thinly sliced
> salt
> freshly ground black pepper
> 150 ml (¼ pint) whipping cream

Preheat the oven to Gas Mark 4/180°C/350°F. Butter a gratin
dish and layer the cheese, garlic, and sweet potato in it, seasoning
as you go. Pour over the cream and bake for an hour.

Helen Cristofoli, London

SWEETCORN

With the best sweetcorn of the year arriving in August and
September, there's no excuse for eating the tinned or frozen
sort. It may be sweet, but it lacks the grassy flavours and firm
texture of the fresh variety. Buy ears of corn from a shop with
a good turnover and eat it the same day, since the sugar starts
turning to starch from the moment it's picked. Or opt for modern
"supersweet" varieties, which are bred to survive shipping better
than most. Taking the corn from the cob is easy. Strip the green
husk and any wispy bits of "silk" from the raw cob. Then just hold
the cob vertically, one end on a board, and use a sharp knife to
cut from top to bottom, taking the kernels off in crumbly strips.

GEORGIA CREAMED CORN
Serves 6
Preparation and cooking time: 1 hour

The careful cutting of the corn here extracts the very most of
the natural milky juices but keeps the nice bobbly texture.
Eat it with grilled meat or fish.

  6-8 ears sweetcorn
  3-4 tbsp butter
  1-2 tbsp caster or granulated sugar

Cut off the very tip of the corn kernels, using the method
described on p.136. When you have worked completely around
the cob, scrape the rest of the corn off. Put this milky pulp in
a pan along with the kernel tips. Add 4 tablespoons of water
to the pan; you may need more later, depending on the starch
content of the corn. Put the saucepan on medium heat and stir
constantly until hot and bubbly. Add the butter and lower the
heat. Cook slowly for at least 30 minutes, stirring occasionally
to keep from sticking. The corn should be thick enough to eat
with a fork. Season, then add the sugar a little at a time until
it tastes sweet enough to you. Serve hot.

Jean Lang, Georgia, USA

CORN POPOVERS

Makes 6-8
Preparation time: 20 minutes
Cooking time: 35 minutes

Popovers are the American answer to Yorkshire puddings –
muffin-sized, crispy, baked batters to have with roast meat.
This version includes sweetcorn and herbs, so you could eat
them on their own too, or with bacon for breakfast. They may
not be for dieters, but they sure are good.

1 ear sweetcorn
110 g (4 oz) strong white flour
30 g (1 oz) polenta or semolina
1 tsp sugar
1/2 tsp salt
220 ml (8 fl oz) milk
2 tbsp melted bacon fat or butter
3 eggs, beaten
3 tbsp coriander, parsley, or chives, chopped
1 chilli, deseeded and finely chopped,
    or a shake of chilli sauce

Preheat the oven to Gas Mark 8/230°C/450°F. Grease a six –
or eight-hole muffin tin. Cut the corn kernels from the cob
(see p.136) and chop them roughly. In a large bowl, mix the
dry ingredients and make a well in the middle. Pour in the milk,
melted butter or bacon fat, and the eggs. Whisk together to make
a smooth batter. Stir in the corn, herbs, and chilli. Pour into the
muffin tin and bake for 15 minutes, then reduce the heat to
Gas Mark 5/190°C/375°F and cook for a further 20 minutes.
Eat straightaway with more butter.

Mark Hebwaite, London

TOMATOES

Every summer I vow to grow my own tomatoes next year.
After all, the choice for the gardener is huge, from tiny
grape-sized tomatoes to yellow pear-shaped beauties, stripy
tigers, and even velvety peach-skinned cultivars. Of course,
looks aren't everything, but most of these heirloom varieties
deliver rich flavour as well, a far cry from the hard pinkish-orange
tomatoes piled up in the supermarket, or even the paltry three
or four "grown for flavour" types available in small, expensive
packets. Those pretty branches of tomatoes on the vine may not
taste any better – the enticing smell comes from the stem not
the tomato, which could be any inferior variety. Look for a deep
colour and types like Gardener's Delight, Marmande, or Roma
instead. Or head for your farmers' market, where an even better
choice may be available.

TOMATO, HERB AND GOAT'S CHEESE TARTS
Serves 4 as a starter or light lunch
Preparation time: 20 minutes
Cooking time: 15–20 minutes

Cherry tomatoes seem to deliver more taste than their larger
mass-produced sisters, and they are good cooked as well as in
salads. Try them in this tomato tart, one of those magic dishes
that looks and tastes a million dollars but is practically effortless
to make. The colour and smell of the creamy, green-flecked
cheese and slightly browned, juicily oozing baby tomatoes are
just fabulous. Better still, there's no tedious lining of tart tins
since the edges of the puff pastry rise up by themselves to make
a proper little pastry case. Really time-pushed cooks could cheat
even more by using a ready-herbed soft cheese.

> 250 g (9 oz) puff pastry
> 1 tbsp red pesto or tomato purée
> 200 g (7 oz) soft goat's cheese
> small bunch each of parsley and chives, chopped
> salt
> freshly ground black pepper
> 300 g (11 oz) cherry tomatoes
> olive oil
> fresh basil leaves

Roll the puff pastry out thinly and, using a saucer as a template,
cut out four 15 cm (6 in) rounds. Put them on a large, damp
baking sheet and, with a sharp knife, gently score around each
round 1 cm (½ in) from the edge. Spread the pesto or tomato
purée over each tart to the scored line. Mix the herbs with the
goat's cheese, along with some seasoning. Pile the cheese on to
the pesto, then scatter the cherry tomatoes on top. Drizzle
a little olive oil on each and cook in the oven for 15–20 minutes.
Scatter with a few ripped basil leaves before serving.

Caroline Marcuse, Pinner, Middlesex

- Gardeners tell me that in our climate cherry tomatoes are a better bet than full size ones for growing outdoors: they've more chance of ripening properly.
- Don't refrigerate tomatoes unless they are really overripe: a few days in a bowl on the kitchen table improves and darkens even pasty Canary Island tomatoes.
- No time to make sauce with a glut of tomatoes? Freeze the tomatoes whole and use them for cooking – the skins slip off easily.

TROUT

Whatever happened to trout with almonds? You don't find it
on hotel menus anymore. Instead it's all seared tuna and griddled
scallops. Well, I say trout is due for a revival. It's cheap, plentiful
and good to eat. For the lucky few, wild trout, freshly caught,
should be best of all. But if, like me, you are stuck with farmed
trout, console yourself: it's unlikely to be muddy tasting, a fault
occasionally found in even the finest angler's catch.

TROUT WITH MUSHROOMS AND OUZO OR PERNOD
Serves 4
Preparation and cooking time: 30 minutes

This gorgeously rich recipe uses Pernod, a drink I can't bear. At student discos it was the only drink sold in glasses rather than disposable cups: apparently it corrodes plastic. What it did to our insides doesn't bear thinking about. In the kitchen, though, aniseedy spirits like Pernod, Ricard, and Ouzo are indispensable, delicious to scent gooseberries, or, in this case, cooking to a fragrantly savoury sauce for fish.

    4 small or 2 medium trout, gutted and cleaned
    seasoned flour
    110 g (4 oz) butter
    225 g (8 oz) button mushrooms, trimmed and sliced
    1 garlic clove, crushed
    2-3 tbsp Ouzo, Pernod, or Pastis
    150 ml (1/2 pint) double cream
    salt
    freshly ground black pepper

Dredge the trout with the seasoned flour. Melt the butter, and fry the fish on both sides until golden brown. Keep warm while you fry the mushrooms and garlic in the trout juices for 2-3 minutes. Stir in the Ouzo, Pernod, or Pastis, and let the liquid bubble rapidly for a few minutes. Stir in the cream and cook until the sauce has reduced to a consistency of thick cream. Season to taste and add a splash more Ouzo or Pernod if necessary. Serve immediately with boiled, buttered potatoes and a crisp green salad.

Michael E. Johnson, Macclesfield

STUFFED TROUT
Serves 2
Preparation time: 20 minutes
Cooking time: 25 minutes

Boneless and easy to eat, this simple stuffed trout slices into
pretty pink-and-green-striped rounds. It's good hot with new
potatoes but excellent cold too, making it perfect for picnics.

> 1 tbsp butter
> 1 medium bag spinach, washed
> salt
> freshly ground black pepper
> freshly ground nutmeg
> 1 tbsp double cream (optional)
> 1 medium trout, filleted
> 3-4 rashers of bacon

Melt the butter in a big pan, and pile in the well-drained spinach.
Keep turning the leaves until well wilted. Remove from the pan,
squeeze out as much moisture as possible, and chop finely.
Season with salt, pepper, and nutmeg; you could add a spoonful
of cream too. Lay the trout fillets out side by side. Put a generous
layer of spinach on one fillet and lay the other on top. Place the
bacon rashers on a board and stretch them out with the back of
a knife. Use them to wrap the fillets. Bake for 25 minutes or so at
Gas Mark 4/180°C/350°F, until cooked through. Slice just before
serving, and serve hot with melted butter or cold with salad and
a dollop of crème fraîche.

Audrey Rotheram, Andover, Hampshire

- Rainbow trout is not native to the UK, but imported
  for farming.
- Check out www.wild-trout.co.uk for lots of information
  on the plethora of different types of wild trout.

VENISON

Tender, succulent farmed venison is in season all year round,
but it's hard to find in the warmer months. Maybe we need
the chill of autumn, the natural game season, to appreciate
the rich flavour and the dark meat. It's certainly one of the
consolations of the end of summer. Low in fat and especially
low in cholesterol, venison tastes like mild beef unless well hung:
about 2¹/₂ weeks is ideal. Most older recipe books deal with game
venison, which has an excellent flavour but is of uncertain age
and can be tough. Get round this by marinating well-hung joints
for as much as 4 days in wine, olive oil, and herbs with
a dash of vinegar or lemon juice, and larding them with pork fat.

Roasting venison:
Choose a well-hung joint of saddle or haunch: save the breast
and shoulder for casseroling. Ask the butcher to lard it or "bard"
it (wrap it) with fat – this is particularly important if you intend
to cook the meat more than medium rare. For pink, tender meat
cook it at Gas Mark 5/190°C/375°F for 17 minutes per 500 g or
15 minutes per 1 lb. Add an extra 7 minutes per 500 g (5 minutes
per 1 lb) for joints under 1.8 kg (4 lb). Allow the meat to rest for
20 minutes or so before carving.

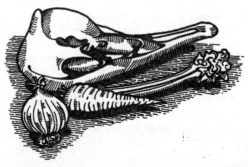

VENISON AND PEAR CASSEROLE
Serves 4
Preparation time: 40 minutes
Cooking time: 2 hours

This is unusual and delicious, unctuous without being dark and
heavy. You can find dried pears in health food shops or fish them
out of a bag of dried fruit salad. They add a delicate honeyed
flavour without being too sweet, but use dried apricots or
prunes if you can't find pears.

olive oil
900 g (2 lb) venison, diced
1 onion, chopped
6 rashers of bacon, chopped
1 carrot, chopped
1 parsnip, chopped
3 sticks celery, chopped
1/2 bottle red wine
1 tsp fresh thyme or 1/2 tsp dried
salt
freshly ground black pepper
300 g (11 oz) shallots or tiny onions
250 g (9 oz) ready-to-eat dried pears
1 wine glass of port

Heat 2 tablespoonfuls of oil and brown the venison a little at
a time. Place in a large casserole dish. Soften the onion and bacon
in a little more oil for a few minutes before adding the carrot,
parsnip, and celery. Cook until the vegetables are softened, then
tip into the casserole with the wine, thyme, and seasoning. Bring
to a simmer and immediately cover and cook in the oven (Gas
Mark 5/190°C/375°F) for 1 1/2 hours. Brown the shallots in a little
oil. Once the casserole has cooked for 1 1/2 hours add the shallots,
pears, and port, and bring back to simmering point. Turn the
oven down to Gas Mark 3/160°C/325°F and cook the casserole
uncovered for a further 30 minutes. Serve with mashed potatoes
or bread. This is best made a day ahead and reheated.

Karen Cann, Sidmouth, Devon

Venison With Onions

Serves 2

Preparation and cooking time: 15 minutes + 1 hour standing

The squeeze of lemon here performs some magical chemical reaction, uniting the flavours to a very savoury whole. Simple, but somehow more than the sum of its parts, it makes a perfect supper for two.

    1 sprig of rosemary, chopped
    1 tbsp olive oil
    2 venison loin steaks, about 200 g (7 oz) each
    1 large onion, sliced
    $^1/_2$ red pepper, finely sliced (optional)
    juice of $^1/_2$ lemon
    salt
    freshly ground black pepper

Mix the rosemary and $^1/_2$ the olive oil. Rub the mixture over the venison and leave to stand for at least 1 hour. Fry the onion briskly for 5 minutes in a frying pan with a heatproof handle, then add the pepper. Place the venison on top and put the pan under a preheated grill. How long you grill depends on the thickness of the steak and your taste: try about 3–6 minutes on each side. Sprinkle over the lemon juice and season.

Trevor Maxfield, Cricklade, Wiltshire

147

VENISON PÂTÉ WITH BRAMBLE SAUCE
Serves 6
Preparation time: 30 minutes + overnight marinating + cooling
time
Cooking time: 1 hour

Now for something to do with the cuts of meat that aren't suitable
for roasting or pan frying. This simple-to-make, gamey, garlicky pâté
is less rich than a normal pâté. Perfect with the fruity bramble
sauce, you could jazz it up with a smidgen of thyme or rosemary.

1 onion, peeled and chopped
6 tbsp butter
320 g (11 oz) lean venison, minced
1 garlic clove, peeled and chopped
150 g (5½ oz) turkey, finely ground
110 ml (4 fl oz) red wine
salt
freshly ground black pepper
50 g (1¾ oz) pine nuts or hazelnuts, toasted

Sauce
225 g (8 oz) blackberries
4 tbsp sugar

Fry the onion in the butter until transparent. Mix in the
venison, garlic, turkey and red wine. Season well – I use about
1½ teaspoonfuls salt and ½ teaspoon pepper. Mix thoroughly,
cover, and refrigerate overnight. Mix again and add the toasted
nuts. Put the mixture in a 450 g (1 lb) terrine dish or loaf tin,
cover with foil, and cook in a preheated oven (Gas Mark 4
180°C/350°F) for 1 hour. Test for doneness by sticking in a
skewer: it should come out clean and hot. Leave to cool, then
chill in the fridge.

For the sauce, cook the blackberries and sugar with
2 tablespoonfuls warm water for about 15 minutes until the
mixture resembles a thin jam. Sieve it, and store the purée in
the fridge until needed. Serve a tablespoonful of sauce with
each slice of pâté.

Marilyn Scott, Bridge of Allan, Scotland

WINTER: LATE DECEMBER TO MID–MARCH

December first, satsumas and nuts, trees of Brussels sprouts, parsnips for roasting. Then it's all over, and there's nearly three months of wintry weather without even Christmas to look forward to. But there's compensation for the bleak days of January and February: spicy, sour Seville oranges to squeeze over fish or delicate slivers of calves' liver, ruby-veined blood oranges, and zesty lemons for February's pancakes.

Winter brings slender stems of vivid, forced rhubarb too – all sophisticated flavour and wild, Barbie, pink colour, followed by greenish-pink outdoor stuff, not so fine but worthwhile all the same, and home grown at least. Late season apples, the "keepers", are good until March, mellowing in storage, but it's now more than ever that we need our imports – the pineapples, mangoes, passionfruit – to balance the wintery stews and casseroles.

It's those bowls of soup, and big pots of stew, which need gratifyingly little last minute attention, that are my favourite part of winter. If ever food was about nurturing, bestowing love and friendship, it's now. Gather round the friends and family, pile the table high. Let it snow, let it snow, let it snow.

BLOOD ORANGES

WINTER BLOOD ORANGE SALAD
Serves 2
Preparation time: 15 minutes

This is a simple, refreshing salad, full of crunch and sassy
flavours. Seville oranges are in the shops at the same time as
blood oranges, and you could use their aromatic sour juice
instead of lemon juice in the dressing. Although supermarkets
sell Seville oranges only in irritatingly large bags, non-marmalade
makers can usually buy single oranges from greengrocers.

    2 blood oranges
    1 small red onion, sliced finely into rings
    1 fennel bulb, sliced finely
    mixed salad leaves

    Dressing:
    3 tbsp extra-virgin olive oil
    1 tbsp fresh lemon juice
    salt
    freshly ground black pepper

Use a small, sharp knife to cut both the peel and the transparent
skin from the orange flesh. (I start by cutting a slice from the top
and bottom of the orange, then cut the peel and skin off in strips,
from top to bottom.) Holding the juicy globe of orange flesh in
your hand, carefully cut the segments of orange out, leaving
behind the membranous skin. Put the orange pieces, onion,
fennel, and salad leaves in a bowl. Mix the dressing ingredients
together and pour over the salad, tossing it gently.

Mrs M. Hill, Bransgore

LIVER WITH ORANGE (FEGATO ALL'ARANCIO)
Serves 2
Preparation and cooking time: 10 minutes

The easiest way to enjoy blood oranges is to make the most
exquisite tomato-coloured juice, but it's also worth using them
in simple recipes like liver in an orange sauce. If you can't get
calves' liver try lambs' liver instead, which is still good although
the texture is coarser. Compensate by crumbling some crisp fried
bacon into the mash.

    small knob of butter
    juice and peel of 1 large blood orange
    2 large slices of calves' liver
    salt
    freshly ground black pepper

Melt the butter in a non-stick frying pan, and add the orange
peel. Raise the heat and add the liver slices, frying for one minute
each side. Add the orange juice and allow to bubble for half
a minute. Season with salt and pepper. Serve with mashed
potatoes and an orange, walnut, and rocket salad, or the
blood orange salad on p.150.

Sarah Boscu, Milan, Italy

Blood Oranges, Grapefruit, and Lychees in Hot Lime Syrup

Serves 4, or more with cake and ice cream
Preparation time: 30 minutes + 15 minutes marinating

Here's a recipe to brighten up a chilly January day – a vividly coloured, lime-zingy fruit salad. It makes the perfect end to an oriental meal, and later in the year you could use ordinary oranges instead of blood ones, although the "blonds" have a less intense taste. This recipe is satisfyingly healthy by itself, or indulgent and dinner-partyish with a slice of orange cake and coconut ice cream.

    2 limes
    110 g (4 oz) sugar
    3–4 blood oranges
    2 pink grapefruit
    450 g (1 lb) fresh or tinned lychees

Peel the limes very thinly and place the peel, sugar, and 300 ml (10 fl oz) water in a saucepan. Bring to the boil, remove from the heat, and leave to infuse for 15 minutes. Remove the peel and add the juice of the limes to the syrup. Peel and segment the grapefruit and oranges, removing all the pith and skin. (To do this, cut a thick slice from the top and bottom of the fruit. Place the fruit on a board and cut off the rest of the peel and the pith in strips, cutting from top to bottom with a serrated knife. Then cut the flesh out from between the leaves of pith that separate each segment.) Drain the tinned lychees, or peel fresh ones. Mix the fruit together, pour over the syrup, and leave it all to marinade. Serve hot or cold, in deep plates or bowls to catch all the copious juice.

Susan Jarman, Llanidloes, Powys

ORANGE AND PARSNIP CAKE

Preparation time: 30 minutes
Cooking time: 90 minutes

Parsnips are far from exotic, but they do give a vaguely eastern
spiciness to this very moist and puddingy cake. It's not as daft as
it sounds, using parsnips in sweet foods: at least one upmarket
restaurant includes parsnip ice cream amongst its desserts.

125 g (4½ oz) butter
140 g (5 oz) soft brown sugar
3 eggs, lightly beaten
grated rind and juice of one blood or ordinary orange
200 g (7 oz) self-raising flour (use half wholemeal
    self-raising if you like)
pinch of salt
2 medium parsnips, finely grated

Preheat the oven to Gas Mark 4/180°C/350°F/. Grease and line
a 1 kg (2 lb) loaf tin. Cream the butter and sugar together in a
food processor until light and fluffy. Add the eggs little by little,
beating well between each addition, then mix in the orange
rind and juice and the flour. Add a pinch of salt, fold in the
parsnips, and scrape the mixture into the loaf tin. Bake for
about 90 minutes, until brown and firm. Cool in the tin.

Sally Logie, Langford, Somerset

- Blood oranges are even higher in vitamin C than other oranges.
- Blood oranges are the result of a natural mutation, which first occurred about 400 years ago, but they were only formally identified at the start of the last century.
- Although the season is said to run until April, blood oranges are hard to find after February.
- Vivid pink-champagne forced rhubarb arrives at the same time as blood oranges: bake it in the oven with sugar and a little grated orange rind, and mix in peeled blood orange segments before serving.
- Sauce Maltaise is hollandaise sauce flavoured with blood orange juice and rind. Unless you can get sour Maltese oranges, add a little lemon or Seville orange juice. Traditionally served with asparagus, it's excellent with fish too.

BRUSSELS SPROUTS

What's in a name? Recently the supermarkets have tried calling
Brussels sprouts "British sprouts". No, not in a bizarre act of
nose-thumbing to the European Commission, but in response
to a campaign by our own growers. I'm not convinced it did
anything for the sprout's image. Think of Cyprus sherry and
Canadian cheddar, neither of them known for their quality.
And Brussels sprouts did after all originate in Belgium. Still,
the New Zealanders renamed the Chinese gooseberry the
kiwi and made it their own, so perhaps this heralds a whole
new era for the humble sprout.

BRUSSELS SPROUTS AND CHESTNUTS
Serves 4
Preparation and cooking time: 30 minutes

Sprouts and bacon is a famous combination. My mother mixes her cooked sprouts with chopped rashers and crispy fried breadcrumbs, and very good they are with the roast turkey. But with more and more vegetarians around, it's useful to have a vegetarian version up your sleeve as well. This mixture of sprouts and chestnuts goes well with eggs or sausages but has enough protein on its own to satisfy non-meat eaters. It tastes delicious too, the mealy nuts mixing perfectly with the nutty, crisp, buttery sprouts. Don't forget the butter. Sprouts are full of healthy vitamins and minerals, and there is even evidence that they protect against bowel cancer, but they are not for dieters, since that strong flavour needs the softening effect of butter or oil to avoid being coarse.

> 450 g (1 lb) small Brussels sprouts
> 170 g (6 oz) chestnuts
> a knob of butter
> salt
> freshly ground black pepper

Score the chestnuts with a sharp knife and roast for 10 minutes at Gas Mark 6/200°C/400°F. Peel a few at a time, keeping the unpeeled ones in the hot oven. Meanwhile, trim the sprouts and cook them in boiling water until just done. Drain and turn them in the butter. Sprinkle over seasoning and the crumbly warm chestnuts and serve.

Noortje Jonker, Reading

LADHERA-STYLE BRUSSELS SPROUTS
Serves 4–6
Preparation time: 10 minutes + 1 hour to cool
Cooking time: 70 minutes

This is an unusual recipe, first discovered whilst on holiday in
Crete, for sprouts cooked slowly in oil. The result is a dish of soft
sprouts bathed in tomato sauce. If you are appalled at the idea
of soggy brassicas, fear not: they are cooked long enough for
any foul, overcooked cabbage smell you might expect to have
dissipated. What remains is a faintly nutty, spicy flavour. It is
rich: I didn't feel the need to put more than a trickle of oil
on at the end. Don't leave it out altogether, though – the
olive flavour is essential.

> 110 ml (4 fl oz) olive oil
> 450 g (1 lb) Brussels sprouts, peeled and trimmed
> 1 large onion, chopped
> 2 large beef tomatoes, skinned and chopped, or a tin
>   of tomatoes (drain off the juice)
> salt
> extra virgin olive oil to serve

Heat the oil in a large lidded pan and sauté the sprouts until
they turn a bright green. Lower the heat a little, add the onion,
cover, and cook until the onion is soft. Add the tomatoes and
a little water, cover again, and cook on a very low heat for at
least 50 minutes. Check occasionally and splash on a little water
if necessary. Season with salt, and continue to cook for another
10 minutes or until the tomatoes have melted to a sauce. Turn
off the heat and leave to cool for an hour or so with the lid on.
Serve lukewarm with extra virgin oil drizzled over.

Paul Bridgewater

PURÉED BRUSSELS SPROUTS
Serves 4
Preparation and cooking time: 20 minutes

Janet Clarke is not a sprouts lover, but she says, "This is one
way to make them not only edible but delicious." These are
truly gourmet sprouts: no cabbage taste, just a sweet nutty
flavour accentuated by all that nutmeg. Since Janet specified
no quantities, I've added mine, as very rough guidance – but
the general idea is to make free with cream and butter.

> 450 g (1 lb) tiny, really fresh Brussels sprouts
> 4 tbsp double cream
> 2 tbsp butter
> at least a quarter of a nutmeg, grated
> salt
> freshly ground black pepper

Boil or steam the sprouts until just done, tip into a processor,
and add large quantities of cream, butter, and seasoning, including
lots of nutmeg. Whizz until pureed and serve immediately.

Janet Clarke, Bath

- Brussels sprouts taste best after the first frosts, like parsnips
  and sloes.
- Sprouts don't keep well: keep them in the fridge and eat them
  within a couple of days.
- Choose the smallest sprouts, which will be tender and milder.
- The trees of sprouts still growing in weird formation on the
  stem can be found at some greengrocers. The sprouts stay
  fresh longer like this, and the bushy leaves at the top can be
  cooked too, although they can be a bit tough.

CLEMENTINES AND SATSUMAS

Clementines and satsumas are so much part of winter and
Christmas. It's not just the juicy flesh, or the fact that they are
so blissfully simple to eat, but the distinctive perfume clinging
to fingertips and scenting clothes that I love. It's easy to see
why fashionable ladies in Imperial China would hold a mandarin
orange so that the fragrance permeated the air around them.

159

PEARS CLEMENTINE

Serves 4
Preparation time: 10 minutes
Cooking time: 1 hour

Unusual and delicious, this is a good recipe for people without
a particularly sweet tooth: my husband adores it. The pepper
seems an odd addition, but think of black pepper on
strawberries, or fashionable chocolate and chilli ice cream.
Spicy heat – and this dish is spicy – goes well with sweet food
and is brilliant after a heavy meal. Eat any leftovers for breakfast.

> 4 unripe pears (or hard cooking pears), peeled, cored,
>   and quartered
> 1–2 tbsp soft brown sugar
> juice of 2 clementines or satsumas
> coarsely ground black pepper

Place the pear quarters in a lidded ovenproof dish. Sprinkle
over the sugar and squeeze over the clementine juice. Grind a
little pepper over the fruits: I found about ½ tsp was right. Put
the lid on the dish and bake at the bottom of a hot oven while
the main meal is being cooked. Check after 20 minutes for
softness, although it could take much longer (but it won't
spoil if kept in the oven a bit too long). Serve warm or cold.
A dollop of ice cream counteracts the heat of the pepper nicely.

Rosie Dean, Saltash, Cornwall

CHOCOLATE-COVERED SATSUMAS
Preparation time: 10 minutes + setting time

Dipping satsuma pieces in molten chocolate turns them into fruit-centred chocolates. They look very impressive but take only minutes to make and are gorgeous with coffee after dinner.

satsumas
plain chocolate

Peel the satsumas and remove as many of the white threads as possible. Pull into segments. Melt some good quality plain chocolate – about 30 g (1 oz) per satsuma. Dunk the segments in the melted chocolate using two teaspoons. Take care not to let any satsuma juice drip into the chocolate or it may turn hard and grainy. Put the segments on greaseproof paper or tin foil until set.

Lorelei Wilmot-Smith, Selby, Yorkshire

- "Mandarin" is a general term covering satsumas, clementines, and also tangerines.
- Shiny, pliable green leaves on clementines don't just look pretty, they indicate freshness.
- Tangelos (e.g. minneolas) are tangerine-grapefruit hybrids. Tangors (e.g. ortaniques) are a cross between a tangerine and an orange. But in France, a "tangerine" is an orange-tangerine cross, called a tangor in the UK.
- Satsumas originate from the Satsuma region of Japan.
- Clemetines are said to be a cross between an Algerian wild orange and a tangerine.
- Mandarins are high in calcium as well as vitamin C.

CRANBERRIES

Cranberries seem gloriously American to me. That's even though we British have taken cranberries to our hearts in the last few years, and come December I have to walk past an acreage of the red beads in punnets at the supermarket before I find the apples and pears. But cranberries shout "Festive Season", with snow-covered log cabins and roaring fires, striped candy canes and home cooking, and all that kitschy stuff which they do so unselfconsciously well Stateside.

Tasted raw, with their mouth-puckering bitter-sour taste, reminiscent of Campari, they aren't an obvious candidate for holiday cheer; especially if, like me, you loathe Campari. But, cooked and sweetened, they have a leafy, spicy flavour that is just right in puddings as well as in meat.

FROZEN CRANBERRY MARTINIS
Makes 6
Preparation time: 5 minutes + freezing time

A brilliantly Christmassy drink, this. A dangerously addictive
confection, not sweet but deliciously fruity. A very grown
up Slush Puppy, in fact, and just looking at the frosty glasses
filled with sparkling magenta crystals makes me want to
throw a party...

> 300 ml (10½ fl oz) cranberry juice
> 200 ml (7 fl oz) frozen vodka
> 2 tbsp dry white vermouth

Mix the ingredients together and pour into a freezer-proof
container. Freeze until slushy: it won't ever freeze solid, so you
could make this a few days ahead. When you're ready to drink,
stir up the slush, or whizz it with a hand-held blender for a
really smooth cocktail. Pour into stemmed glasses and get
stuck in straight away.

Gaetana Trippetti, Stockport, Cheshire

CRANBERRY AND HAZELNUT TART
Serves 6
Preparation time: 30 minutes
Cooking time: 35–40 minutes

You can eat this red-dimpled tart warm, but I think it's best at room temperature when the cranberry has mellowed a bit to give a pleasing sharp contrast to the sweet, nutty filling.

300 g (10½ oz) sweet shortcrust pastry
100 g (3½ oz) shelled hazelnuts
100g (3½ oz) butter
100g (3½ oz) caster sugar
2 eggs, beaten
25 g (1 oz) plain flour
3 tbsp cranberry, bramble, or redcurrant jelly
150 g (5½ oz) cranberries
icing sugar

Preheat the oven to Gas Mark 5/190°C/375°F/, and put a baking sheet in. Line a 23 cm (9 in) flan tin with the pastry, prick the base, and put in the fridge to rest. Toast the hazelnuts in the oven or in a dry frying pan until golden brown, then tip into a tea towel and rub off the skins, if there are any. Then grind the toasted nuts in a food processor until finely chopped. Beat the butter and sugar until pale, then beat in the eggs little by little. Stir in the nuts and the flour. Spread the red jelly over the pastry base, followed by the hazelnut mixture. Sprinkle over the cranberries and gently press them into the nut mixture. Place in the oven on the hot baking sheet and bake for 35–40 minutes or until the tart is browned and firm to the touch. Leave to cool for at least 5 minutes before dusting with icing sugar and serving.

Gill Douglas, Penrith

GINGER

Delicious, spicy, fresh ginger – crucial to Asian, Indian, and African food, as well as (dried) in English gingerbread and spiced beef – has one failing. It's hopelessly tricky to measure. Recipes often call for a length ("2 in fresh ginger"), which can be infuriating when faced with a particularly odd shaped piece. And since fresh ginger varies considerably in pungency, measurements in teaspoonfuls or by weight aren't failsafe either. You just have to use your judgement. My solution is to imagine an average diameter of around 3 cm (a bit more than an inch), and adjust the length I use accordingly – more for a thin root, less for a fat one. Taste the mixture to check the flavour if you can; otherwise be cool. A little more or less gingery really won't matter.

SEA BASS WITH GINGER AND GARLIC
Serves 2
Preparation and cooking time: 30 minutes

I love this recipe. It's the perfect special supper for two, packed
with gorgeous oriental flavours and almost as good made with
(much cheaper) trout. Eat it with rice – plain or flavoured with
coconut milk.

> a 400 g (1 lb) sea bass (or two trout), gutted and descaled
> but with the head left on
> salt
> freshly ground black pepper
> vegetable oil
> 4 x ½ cm (¼ in) slices root ginger, peeled
> 2 or 3 cloves garlic, thinly sliced
> 1 Chinese cabbage or 225 g (8 oz) mangetout
> Thai fish sauce

Make three diagonal cuts on each side of the fish, and season
liberally with salt and pepper. Pour the oil into a large frying
pan to a depth of 3 mm (⅛ in). Fry the fish briskly until crisp
and brown on both sides, and nearly cooked through. Remove
from the pan and keep warm. In the same pan, fry the ginger
and garlic until lightly browned. Scoop out and keep warm.
Raise the heat and stir fry the cabbage or mangetout. Season
with a good slug of Thai fish sauce, salt, and pepper, and add
a splash of water to loosen things up. Dish the vegetables out
on to a warmed oval plate, and top with the fish. Sprinkle
over the garlic and ginger garnish.

Choo Lim, Rotherham

LENTIL AND GINGER BROTH
Serves 2-3
Preparation and cooking time: 1 hour

This Nigerian soup is filling and sinus-clearingly spicy, making an excellent cold cure. It is admittedly somewhat ascetic: if I'm feeling like something a little richer I make it with stock instead of water and top it with yogurt and coriander leaves.

  2 tbsp olive oil
  2 onions, chopped
  2-3 cloves of garlic, crushed
  1 or more fresh chillis, chopped
  5 cm (2 in) fresh ginger, grated
  2-3 tbsp fresh coriander root (or stems), chopped
  100 g (4 oz) green lentils
  1 litre (1³/₄ pints) water
  lemon juice
  salt
  freshly ground black pepper

In a large saucepan fry the onions and garlic in the olive oil until soft but not browned, then add the chilli, ginger, and coriander. Add the water and lentils and bring to the boil. Lower the heat and simmer for about 45 minutes or until the lentils are soft. Add lemon juice to taste and plenty of salt and ground black pepper.

Venetia Harwood Pearce, RAF Cyprus

GINGER AND COCONUT MACKEREL
Serves 3-4
Preparation and cooking time: 80 minutes

This is easy to make and a great way of using mackerel, one of
the few fish that remains a sustainable catch. Eat it hot with rice,
or cold as a creamy salad sprinkled with coriander leaves.

    4 small or 2 large mackerel
    1 medium onion, halved and thinly sliced
    1 tbsp vegetable oil
    400 ml (14 fl oz) coconut milk
    2 tbsp grated fresh ginger
    2-4 garlic cloves, chopped
    ½ tsp salt
    1 tbsp crème fraîche

Clean, rinse, and wipe the mackerel dry. Place under a medium
grill for 15-20 minutes, turning them half way through the
cooking time, which will depend on the size of the fish. Remove
the fish from the heat and allow them to sit until cool enough
to handle. Remove the skin and bones. Try to keep the fish in
large chunks rather than flakes. Meanwhile, fry the onion in the
oil until softened but not coloured. Empty the coconut milk into
a pan, add the ginger, and bring it all slowly to boiling point.
Add the onion and garlic and simmer gently for about
20 minutes. Stir in the salt, then add the fish and heat through.
Remove from the heat, add the crème fraîche, and stir gently.

John Smart, Waterlooville, Hampshire

FRESH GINGER GINGERBREAD

Makes 8-10 pieces
Preparation time: 20 minutes + 10 minutes cooling time
Cooking time: 45-60 minutes

Try this moist, squidgy gingerbread after a wet spring walk.
Spiced up with fresh ginger, you could add some chopped
candied ginger to the mixture too. It's also good enough to eat
warm as a pudding, with cream and poached rhubarb.

210 g (7 oz) plain flour
1 tsp bicarbonate of soda
pinch of salt
115 g (4 oz) butter
125 ml (4½ fl oz) water
100 g (3½ oz) soft brown sugar
4 tbsp golden syrup
4 tbsp black treacle
1 egg
55 g (2 oz) fresh ginger, finely grated
honey or ginger jam

Heat the oven to Gas Mark 4/180°C/350°F. Grease and line a
23 x 23 cm (9 x 9 in) tin. Sift together the flour, bicarbonate
of soda, and salt. In a pan, heat the butter and water gently until
the butter is melted. Mix the sugar, syrup, black treacle, egg,
and ginger together. Add the flour and the butter mixtures.
Mix together well and scrape into the cake tin. Bake for about
45-60 minutes, until a skewer inserted in the centre comes out
without uncooked mixture on it. Allow to cool for 10 minutes
in the tin, then turn out and peel off the paper. Brush the top
with the honey or warmed ginger jam and continue cooling
the right way up. Cut into 8-10 pieces.

Suzie Hudson, West Runton, Cromer, Norfolk

GINGER AND APRICOT PORRIDGE
Serves 1
Preparation time: 10 minutes

Ginger is said to stimulate the circulation, soothe the digestion, and purify the blood. If you've ever had carrot and ginger juice you'll know it's an eye-opening start to the day, although on a chilly morning porridge is more sustaining. The problem is, many people find porridge disgusting without lashings of golden syrup and cream. Try this fruity, spicy version – delicious without piling on fat and sugar.

> 1 bowl porridge oats
> milk or water
> 1 tsp good quality apricot preserve
> 1–2 tsp mild yoghurt
> 1 tsp fresh ginger, finely grated

Make the porridge using milk, water, or half and half. Stir in the other ingredients and eat straight away.

Pam Pointer, Salisbury, Wiltshire

- Never buy wizened-looking ginger: it should always be plump and tight-skinned.
- Store ginger in the freezer. It keeps there indefinitely. Don't defrost it, but grate it from frozen; use the coarse side of a box grater. There's no need to peel it first.
- The large bulbous, irregular rhizomes of fresh ginger (also known as "root ginger" or "green ginger") are called "hands".

HOMEMADE CHRISTMAS PRESENTS

Let's get one thing straight: making delicious goodies for
presents, using pricey first class ingredients, is not a cheapskate
option. Factor in the cost of your time as well – and you aren't
cheap – and these things start looking very pricey. But they
do provide welcome relief from the pervasive commercialism
of the season, and, of course, they taste better too.

PANETTONE
Makes 4 small panettone
Preparation time: 40 minutes + about 2 hours rising
Cooking time: 35–40 minutes

This version of panettone, the gorgeously fragrant Italian yeasted
cake, is a Boxing Day breakfast tradition for many of Janet's
friends. It looks especially pretty wrapped in cellophane (from
florists or paper shops) and tied with raffia and a twist of dried
orange peel. It doesn't keep brilliantly though, so if you want
to make yours more than a couple of days ahead, freeze it.
If you can't get fresh yeast, use a sachet of easy-blend yeast
instead, and just stir it into all the flour along with the salt.
If you do this, there's no need to mix the flour and milk:
use all the milk to infuse the saffron.

675 g (1½ lbs) plus 8 tbsp unbleached white bread flour
pinch salt
30 g (1 oz) fresh yeast
500 ml (18 fl oz) milk
pinch saffron
225 g (8 oz) unsalted butter
3 whole eggs plus 3 yolks
1 tsp vanilla extract
4 tbsp caster sugar
110 g (4 oz) sultanas
225 g (8 oz) whole mixed candied peel cut into small dice
zest of 2 oranges and 2 lemons

Put the 675 g (1½ lbs) flour into a large bowl, add the salt and
set on one side. Heat the milk to blood heat, pour about half
onto the yeast, and cream thoroughly. Add the 8 tbsp flour, mix
well, cover loosely with cling film, and leave until well risen.
Crumble the saffron into the remaining milk, add the butter,
and heat very gently until the butter is melted. Beat the eggs, add
the vanilla extract and the sugar, pour into the flour in the large
bowl, add the milk (stirring well) and the yeast mixture, and
mix well together. Knead the batter-like dough by slapping it
with your hands until smooth and stretchy or knead it for a
couple of minutes in a tabletop mixer, using the dough hook.
Cover loosely with cling film and leave to rise until doubled in
size. Then knead again, adding in the sultanas, candied peel, and
fruit zest. Preheat the oven to Gas Mark 5/190°C/375°F. Divide
the dough into portions and put it into four 450 g (1 lb) loaf
tins or 15 cm (6 in) round, deep soufflé dishes or cake tins.
Leave until doubled in size, then bake for 20 minutes. Take out
of the oven and turn each panettone round, middles to sides,
and the whole tray front to back. Replace in the oven, covering
them with a sheet of greaseproof paper, and bake for a further
15–20 minutes (add a total of 30 minutes for round tins).
Cool on a wire rack, and serve plain with coffee or spread
with butter or marscapone cheese.

Janet Clarke, Bath

Biscotti di Prato

Makes about 60
Preparation time: 30 minutes
Cooking time: 35–45 minutes

These biscotti – Italian twice-cooked biscuits – are delicious.
They make a good present, especially if you pile them in a pretty
jar – French preserving jars are great – interleaved with gold
tissue paper. Eat them after dinner with coffee, or, better still,
have a glass of dessert wine (classically vin santo) to dip them in.

> 225 g (8 oz) whole unpeeled almonds
> 500 g (1 lb 2 oz) white unbleached flour
> 1 tsp baking powder
> pinch salt
> 500 g (1 lb 2 oz) caster sugar
> 4 eggs, beaten
> grated zest of 1 orange
> 1 tsp vanilla extract

Preheat the oven to Gas Mark 5/190°C/375°F. Bake the almonds
in the oven for about 5 minutes, until brittle and very lightly
coloured (break one in half to see), then cool and chop roughly.
Sift the flour, baking powder, and salt into a large bowl, and add
the sugar, eggs, orange zest, vanilla extract, and nuts, mixing well.
Divide the mixture into two and shape it into long, thin logs
(think of a slightly flattened cucumber) on a baking tray lined
with non-stick paper. Bake for 25–30 minutes until firm. Remove
from the oven, and lower the heat to Gas Mark 2/150°C/300°F.
Leave the biscotti loaves to cool slightly, then cut into diagonal
fingers, spread them out on the tray, and put them back in the
oven for 10–15 minutes to dry out completely.

Janet Clarke, Bath

CHOCOLATE TRUFFLES
Makes about 30
Preparation time: 1 hour + setting time

This recipe is inspiringly simple, so you can use your own flavourings to make your own versions. The trendiest are chopped red chilli, cardamom, or lavender flowers, but old favourites like stem ginger or orange liqueur are hard to beat. White chocolate truffles taste great with a tablespoonful of finely ground coffee beans added to the mix. Do use really good chocolate: there are lots of excellent plain versions about. My favourite white is Green and Black's creamy, vanilla-seed-freckled version.

> 225 g (8 oz) 70% cocoa solids plain chocolate
> or
> 300 g (11 oz) good quality white chocolate
> flavourings of your choice (see above)
> 175 ml (6 fl oz) double cream
> icing sugar, cocoa powder, or more chocolate to coat

Melt the chocolate into the cream, either in a pan over a low heat or by blasting it for 1 minute in the microwave. Stir in any flavourings that take your fancy. Allow to cool completely in a cool room, but ideally not in the fridge. With your hands dusted with icing sugar, take small teaspoonfuls of the mixture and shape it into balls, or what you will. Coat the balls with cocoa and chill or freeze. Dip the truffles in melted chocolate to coat them – use cocktail sticks and let them set on baking parchment. Alternatively, just recoat them with cocoa. Pack them in boxes lined with tissue paper.

Anne Gough, Clavering, Essex

NOODLES

When it's cold and damp outside, my nose is blocked,
my tastebuds dampened, and my spirits low, I make an instant
noodle soup. It's nothing more than boiling water poured over
dried noodles and a crumbled tom yum stock cube (from
oriental foodshops), covered for 4 minutes, then stirred, with a
few coriander leaves if I'm feeling posh. The first mouthful brings
tears to the eyes, then the searingly hot and sour liquid clears the
sinuses and opens the pores; think sauna from the inside out – an
Oriental spa cure. Meanwhile, the carbohydrate-rich noodles
soothe and nourish. Suddenly life doesn't seem so grey, and I
have a virtuous glow as this doesn't break the New Year diet.

SQUID WITH SPINACH EGG NOODLES
Serves 4
Preparation and cooking time: 20 minutes

This is great to throw together after work, and tastes healthy
and fresh. Don't stint on the garlic or chilli since their flavours
are an important part of the dish, but plain egg noodles will
do fine if you can't get the pretty green spinach ones.

   280 g (10 oz) spinach egg noodles
   3 tbsp olive oil
   1 mild chilli, deseeded and finely chopped
   3 fat garlic cloves, finely chopped
   900 g (2 lb) small squid, cleaned and cut into rings
   a handful of parsley, chopped
   salt
   200 g (7 oz) young spinach, washed
   sesame oil

Cook the noodles according to the packet instructions.
Meanwhile, put the olive oil in a large heavy-bottomed frying
pan and heat gently. Add the chilli and garlic and cook for
2 minutes. Stir in the squid, half the parsley, and a good pinch
of sea salt. When the squid is just starting to cook, add the
spinach and cover the pan. After a minute, stir and taste.
When the spinach is starting to wilt, and the squid barely
cooked, add the rest of the parsley. Toss the hot noodles
with a few drops of sesame oil and serve alongside the squid,
or mix everything together in a green and white melange.

George Marriott, Burgh le Marsh, Lincolnshire

AROMATIC VERMICELLI SOUP
Serves 2
Preparation and cooking time: 45 minutes

This has a subtle but lingering flavour, smokey and garlicky, best sipped slowly. It uses my favourite noodles, the translucent white rice noodles that have an ethereal quality. Most supermarkets stock them, or try a Chinese supermarket for a bewildering selection.

> 5 dried Chinese mushrooms (I used shitake)
> 40 g (1½ oz) clear vermicelli or cellophane rice noodles
> 1 tbsp vegetable oil
> 2 garlic cloves, finely chopped
> 3 Chinese leaves, cut across into 2 cm (1 in) pieces
> salt
> a few torn coriander leaves

Soak the mushrooms in 425 ml (¾ pint) of boiling water for 30 minutes. Meanwhile, soak the noodles in cold water, draining them when the 30 minutes is up. Slice the mushrooms finely (keep their soaking water). Heat the oil in a saucepan and cook the garlic, without browning, for a minute or two. Add the mushrooms and cook, stirring for a couple of minutes more. Stir in the mushroom water and Chinese leaves, bring to the boil, and simmer for 5 minutes. Add the noodles and cook for 1 minute. Season, divide between two bowls, and scatter over the coriander leaves.

Lai Chee Choy-Ryves, Callington, Cornwall

ORANGES

After all that rich Christmas food, oranges are just what I feel like eating. Juicy, fragrant, sweet and sour, they blast away the winter blues, not to mention post-party hangovers.

SPICED ORANGE AND GRAPEFRUIT SALAD
Serves 4-6
Preparation time: 20 minutes

Oranges work brilliantly in savoury dishes, like this gorgeous salad. The green, red, and orange colour combination is ravishing to jaded eyes, even if you can't get a pomegranate. Don't leave out the allspice; its mellow spiciness is unusually good here.

85 g (3 oz) rocket
5 large oranges
2 red grapefruits
1 red onion, finely sliced
1 tsp allspice berries, coarsely ground
$\frac{1}{3}$ tsp black pepper, coarsely ground
1 tsp sea salt
$1\frac{1}{2}$ tbsp olive oil
1 tsp Dijon mustard
seeds from 1 pomegranate

Spread the rocket out on a large serving plate. With a sharp serrated knife, slice the peel and membrane from the oranges and grapefruits. Holding the peeled fruit over a bowl, carefully cut out the wedges of flesh from the remaining membrane. Spread the chunks of orange and grapefruit over the rocket (keep the juice), followed by the sliced onion. Sprinkle with the ground allspice, black pepper, and sea salt. Whisk together the olive oil and mustard and a tablespoon of juice from the fruit. Taste, and add more juice if the mustard taste is too strong. Trickle the dressing over the salad, then sprinkle over the pomegranate seeds. Serve immediately.

Marie-Charlotte Jenkinson, Stockholm

ICED ORANGE TERRINE
Serves 8
Preparation time: 30 minutes + freezing time

Moulded into an impressive looking terrine, this is blissfully
easy to make, and easier still to eat. Add a trickle of bitter
chocolate sauce for chocolate orange nirvana, or eat it with
the baked oranges on p.200.

> 2 eggs, separated
> 110 g (4 oz) caster sugar
> grated rind and juice of 2 large oranges
> 300 ml (½ pint) double cream, lightly whipped
> mint leaves

Whisk the egg whites until stiff, then gradually whisk in half
the sugar. Put the orange rind, egg yolks, and the remaining sugar
into another bowl and whisk until thick and pale. Whisk the
orange juice into the whipped cream. Fold the cream into the
egg yolk mixture, then fold in the egg whites. Turn into a 1 litre
(2 pint) loaf tin, lined with cling film. Cover and freeze until firm.
Turn out on to a serving plate and decorate with mint leaves.

Clare Francis, Andover, Hampshire

BAKED ORANGES
Serves 4, or 6 with ice cream
Preparation time:

When a plain orange salad seems just too chilly and ascetic, these boozy, caramelised baked oranges make a perfect light pudding.

    4–6 sweet, juicy oranges
    juice of 1 lemon
    60 g (2 oz) soft brown sugar
    30 g (1 oz) butter
    1 wine glass of sweet sherry

Peel the oranges, removing all the pith, including the centre core, and slice thinly. Arrange the slices so that they overlap in a shallow ovenproof dish. Sprinkle on the lemon juice. Dredge with the sugar, dot with the butter, and pour over the sherry. Bake at Gas Mark 6/200°C/400°F for 15–20 minutes until the oranges are lightly browned.

Jo Boswell, Norwich

PANCAKES

A well-proved frying pan is the best non-stick surface you can
get for pancakes. To make your pan pancake-perfect, dredge
the flat surface of the pan with table salt. Pour over vegetable
oil to moisten. Heat until smoking, then take a very fat wodge
of kitchen paper, and scour the inside of the pan vigorously,
being careful not to let your skin touch the hot salt or pan.
Finally tip away the oily salt, removing all traces with more
kitchen paper. If you don't have time to do this, supermarkets
stock perfectly OK ready-made pancakes that only need heating
through to serve with sugar and lemon. Try rolling them round
a filling of defrosted, drained, frozen spinach mixed with
melted butter and nutmeg, covering with cheese sauce
and parmesan, and heating through in the oven until
bubbling and golden brown.

PUDLA (CHICK PEA FLOUR PANCAKES)
Makes 6
Preparation and cooking time: 30 minutes

These are a vegetarian Indian speciality – spicy and delicious, especially if you roll them with plain yoghurt. You could add some chopped tomatoes to the batter too, but either way they need only some salad and chutney to make them into a meal.

175 g (6 oz) chick pea flour ("besan" or "gram" flour)
$\frac{1}{2}$ tsp salt
$\frac{1}{2}$ tsp sugar
1 tbsp lemon juice
$\frac{1}{4}$ tsp turmeric (optional)
$\frac{1}{2}$ tsp cayenne pepper (optional)
1 small red onion, very finely chopped
2.5 cm (1 in) ginger, finely minced
1 garlic clove, finely minced
2 tbsp fresh coriander leaves, chopped
vegetable oil

Place the chick pea flour in a large mixing bowl, and gradually stir in enough cold water to make a smooth batter with the consistency of single cream. Add all the other ingredients, mixing well. Set the mixture aside for 15 minutes. Heat a non-stick frying pan with $\frac{1}{2}$ tablespoonful of vegetable oil, over a medium heat. Pour in a half ladle of batter, and tilt the pan quickly to spread the mixture (as if making a crêpe). Cook for about 90 seconds, until the underside of the pancake is golden. Turn over and cook for 1 minute. Serve with plain yoghurt and, perhaps, some salad.

Chandy Taank, South Harrow, Middlesex

STICKY TOFFEE PANCAKES
Makes 12 Scotch pancakes
Preparation and cooking time: 40 minutes

Divinely sweet and rich, these are small, thick, Scotch-style
pancakes. I like to add a few extra chopped dates to the batter
and pass round some lemon or, better still, Seville orange
quarters, to squeeze over.

> *Toffee sauce:*
> 175 g (6 oz) soft brown sugar
> 200 g (7 oz) unsalted butter
> 280 ml (½ pint) double cream
>
> 170 g (6 oz) pitted dates, diced
> 1 tsp bicarbonate of soda
> 280 ml (½ pint) soured cream
> 3 large eggs, separated
> 250 g (9 oz) self-raising flour, sieved
> 90 g (3 oz) soft brown sugar
> butter

To make the sauce, heat all the ingredients in a pan, without
boiling, until the butter has melted. Simmer for 3–4 minutes to
thicken. Keep warm while you make the pancakes. Put the dates
in a bowl and pour over 250 ml (9 fl oz) of boiling water. Stir in
the bicarbonate of soda, and allow to stand for 5 minutes. Drain
the dates and put in a food processor with the sour cream. Blitz
until smooth and then add the egg yolks. Beat well. Combine the
flour and sugar in a bowl and make a well in the centre. Pour the
date mixture into the well, mixing everything together to make
a smooth batter. Whisk the egg whites to soft peaks, and fold,
half at a time, into the date batter. Heat a large frying pan and
melt a small knob of butter. Pour a heaped tablespoon of the
batter into the pan, cook until bubbles form on the surface, and
flip the pancake over to cook the other side. Repeat with the rest
of the batter. Serve with the toffee sauce and vanilla ice cream.

Jossie Parker, Huddersfield

PIGEON

Woodpigeon is available all year round, but it's especially welcome early in the year, when the best of the game is over and the spring lamb hasn't arrived. The dark, well-flavoured meat is low fat too. Very young birds can be roasted whole, or their breasts can be quickly fried like fillet steak. However, unless you are in receipt of a bird in full feather it's hard to be sure of the age, so gently casseroling them is a better option.

There are woodpigeons fluttering in the trees behind my house. I've resisted the temptation to fetch the shotgun, although I take an Alan Clark-like view that game is fair game, so to speak, when it comes to eating – far more so than farmed meat, which never has a chance. But a butcher who deals with game can, with a day's notice, provide a nicely plucked and drawn bird, ready to cook, for around £1.30. So why would I want to get in a messy flurry of down and entrails?

If you do get birds in full feather, though, you will be able to gauge their age properly. Readers sent lots of tips: a young woodpigeon won't have developed the white neck ring of an adult and will have a flexible beak. The breastbone too will be supple, which is a sign even on a prepared bird that it's young enough to roast whole, barded with plenty of bacon to stop the lean meat drying out. If you want to cook just the breasts, these can be cut off the whole bird, and the feathers and skin ripped off in one, which is fast although of course the unplucked carcasse is then no use for stock.

Terrine of Pigeon
Serves
Preparation time: 40 minutes + 2–3 days marinating
Cooking time: 2 hours

Mrs. Brew's pâté or terrine is richly flavoured with a lovely
texture – smooth with bits. I had my doubts about the vinegar
in the marinade, but in fact it gives a tang that balances the
gaminess of the pigeon. Next time I make it I'm tempted to add
a few crushed juniper berries, but then why mess with
something so simple and good?

> 4 pigeons (or 3 if they're very plump)
> 250 ml (9 fl oz) red wine
> 125 ml (4 fl oz) mild cider vinegar
> 1 bay leaf
> sprig of thyme
> 1 tsp grated nutmeg
> olive oil
> 300 g (11oz) green streaky bacon, rinds removed
> thick slice of bread
> milk
> 300 g (11oz) minced pork
> salt
> freshly ground black pepper
> small glass of brandy

Slice the pigeon breasts from the breastbone and use a sharp
knife or a pair of scissors to strip the rest of the flesh from the
carcasses. Discard the skin. Place the pigeon meat, red wine,
cider vinegar, bay leaf, thyme, and nutmeg in a bowl. Cover
and refrigerate for 2–3 days. Lightly oil a 500 g (1 lb) loaf tin
or terrine dish and line it with the bacon. Cut the pigeon breasts
into thin slices, and mince or finely chop the rest of the pigeon
meat. Cut the crusts off the bread and soak it in milk. Squeeze
it out and mix it in with the pork and all the pigeon. Season
carefully: the only way to be sure you've got it right is to fry
a little of the mixture and taste it. Place the seasoned mixture
in the bacon-lined dish, pressing down well. Pour over the
brandy. Cover with more bacon. Bake in a preheated oven
(Gas Mark 3/170°C/325°F) for 2 hours. Cool in the tin. Turn out
and serve in slices with bread and chutneys.

Simone Brew, Shenley, Hertfordshire

PIGEON WITH BLACK PUDDING
Serves 4-6
Preparation time: 30 minutes
Cooking time: 90 minutes

This is a fantastic recipe. The addition of black pudding is an ace idea. It's unidentifiable in the final dish but melts into the sauce, making it dark, rich, and delicious. I reckon it would be a good way of enriching all sorts of meat stews.

> 6 pigeons
> 2 tbsp oil
> 2 onions, finely chopped
> 1 large garlic clove, finely chopped
> 3 fat slices of black pudding
> 1 large tin chopped tomatoes
> 1 tbsp flour
> red wine or pigeon stock
> salt
> freshly ground black pepper

Slice the breasts off the pigeon (or ask the butcher to do this) and cut each breast into two or three pieces. Keep the carcasses to make game stock. Heat the oil in a large frying pan and fry the pigeon pieces gently, a few at a time, to brown them. Put the pieces into a large casserole dish. In the frying pan, cook the onions and garlic until softened. Add them to the pigeon pieces, followed by the chunks of black pudding. Liquidise the tomatoes with the flour, and pour into the casserole dish. Add enough wine or stock to just about cover the pigeon: push the pieces down if necessary. Put in a slow oven (Gas Mark 1/2/130°C/250°F) for about 90 minutes, until tender. Adjust the seasoning.
Eat with mashed potatoes.

Rupert Godfrey, King's Lynn, Norfolk

POTATOES

Where would British food be without potatoes? This South
American tuber is an indispensable part of Northern European
cookery. It's an extraordinarily adaptable vegetable, good on its
own or as a vehicle for other flavours, useful as a thickener in
soups and casseroles, and useful in peasant food as in cream rich
haute cuisine. Potatoes are either "floury", the sort that are good
for mashing, or "waxy", like new potatoes, good for salads
or eating boiled with butter and herbs. Shops and supermarkets
are offering a better and better choice, so we can be picky about
variety too now. Check the names and compare the flavours so
that you can build a list of favourites: I like King Edward or Maris
Piper for baking and mashing, and Anya or Pink Fir Apple for
salads. If you eat a lot of potatoes, it's worth picking up a sack
of potatoes from a farm. They're good value, and their mucky,
earth-covered state is a positive advantage. Unlike the spookily
pristine supermarket offerings, these potatoes keep well in a
dark place, and the flavour is better too. Worth getting your
hands dirty for.

POTATO "CHEESE CAKES"
Makes 10
Preparation time: 40 minutes
Cooking time: 30 minutes

These are cheesecakes without cheese – moist, lemony curd
tarts made lighter, and given, it's true, a faintly cheesy flavour
by the potato.

> 225 g (8 oz) old potatoes, peeled
> 375 g (13 oz) shortcrust pastry
> 110 g (4 oz) butter
> 2 eggs, lightly beaten
> 110 g (4 oz) caster sugar
> 2 level tbsp self-raising flour
> juice and rind of 1 lemon
> 110 g (4 oz) currants

Boil and sieve the potatoes. Leave to cool. Roll out the pastry,
not too thinly, and use it to line muffin tins. Leave to rest in the
fridge. Cream the butter, then mix in the eggs. Add the potatoes,
sugar, flour, lemon juice and rind, and mix well, ideally with an
electric hand whisk. Gently stir in the currants so as to keep
them whole. Fill the muffin tins with the runny and rather
curdled-looking mixture. Bake for 30 minutes at Gas Mark 4
180°C/350°F until a pale golden colour. Eat while still just warm,
or at room temperature.

Mrs Margaret Bell, Towcester, Northamptonshire

BACON, POTATO AND CIDER CASSEROLE
Serves 4
Preparation time: 20 minutes
Cooking time: 13/4 hours

There's something about potatoes, bacon, and onion. Bake them
slowly together so that the potato is melting and infused with
porkiness and you have the perfect comfort food. Cheap too,
and pretty healthy. What more could you want? There are lots
of versions around. Some layer the ingredients with milk or white
sauce, some with cheese or ricotta. I love this version, cooked
in cider. The flavour is subtle, but splashing on a good slug of
the amber nectar at the end turns the dish into a feast – think
of pork in cider.

> butter
> 900 g (2 lb) potatoes, peeled and thinly sliced
> 2 medium onions, thinly sliced
> 150 g (6 oz) smoked bacon, chopped small
> salt
> freshly ground black pepper
> 6 tbsp dry cider

Lightly grease a deep, lidded casserole with butter. Arrange layers
of potato, onion, and bacon in the casserole, seasoning with a
little salt and a lot of pepper as you go. Finish with a layer of
potato and dot with butter. Sprinkle with the cider. Cover and
bake for 90 minutes at Gas Mark 7/220°C/325°F. Remove the
lid and continue to bake for 15 minutes or so. When it is done,
if you like, splash another few spoonfuls of cider on top before
serving it with vegetables or salad.

Joan Kalcev, Rochdale

● Weight for weight, potatoes contain more vitamin C
than apples.

Sea Bass

With its milky-white flesh and superb flavour, sea bass is a real delicacy, and the perfect antidote to too much heavy food. You don't want to do too much to it: just plain grilled it's delicious. Don't overcook though! Press the skin of the bass with your fingertips as it cools. As soon as you can feel the moist flakes of fish sliding apart, it's done.

SEA BASS FILLETS WITH TOMATO AND OLIVE OIL
Serves 4
Preparation and cooking time: 25 minutes

Although I generally prefer to cook sea bass whole, sometimes easy-to-serve, easy-to-eat fillets are the thing, especially if you're dealing with a very large fish. Try this gorgeous method of bathing the fish in an unctuous sauce of tomatoey, garlicky, olive oil. It's one of those dishes where the results far exceed the effort spent and is worth trying with more humble fish as well. Don't forget lots of mashed potato for all that sauce.

> 2 large ripe tomatoes, skinned
> 6 tbsp extra virgin olive oil
> 2 garlic cloves, crushed
> 2 tbsp parsley, finely chopped
> 1 tsp dried chilli flakes, or a fresh chilli, chopped
> ½ glass white wine
> salt
> freshly ground black pepper
> 4 fillets of sea bass

Cut the tomatoes in half and scoop out the seeds. Dice the flesh neatly. Heat the oil in wide shallow pan, and add the garlic, parsley, and chilli flakes. Cook for 2 minutes, then add the tomato and cook for another 2 minutes. Add the wine, raise the heat, and bubble for 2 minutes. Season, reduce the heat, and lay the bass fillets, skin side up, in the pan. Cover and cook for 5 minutes. Serve the fillets, skin side down, with the sauce poured over.

John Golding, Huntingdon

WHOLE SEA BASS WITH GINGER AND GARLIC
Serves 2
Preparation time: 10 minutes
Cooking time: 10–15 minutes

Ginger garlic stuffing adds a subtle oriental note to this dish,
without overpowering the fish. I've always got satsumas or
clementines kicking around in the winter, and squeezing one
or two over the top adds a gentle citrus note, and if you're
lucky some yummy, sticky pan juices.

    2 tbsp fresh ginger, grated
    3 garlic cloves, crushed
    salt
    freshly ground black pepper
    2 small or 1 medium sea bass, gutted and scaled
    1–2 satsumas
    1 tbsp olive oil

Heat the oven to Gas Mark 6/200°C/400°F. Mix the ginger and
garlic and season. Stuff the fish with this mixture, and place in
a baking dish. Squeeze the juice from the satsuma and mix with
the oil. Pour over the fish. Bake for 10 minutes for small fish,
15 minutes for a medium one.

Isabel Sioufi, South Croydon

- Buy only farmed bass or line-caught wild sea bass: vast trawler nets are responsible for appalling environmental damage and large-scale dolphin death.
- Never buy anything labelled "Chilean sea bass" – it's likely to be the Patagonian toothfish, which has been fished almost to extinction.
- The minimum size for British wild sea bass is 37.5 cm (14¾ in) long – so if it's smaller, it's probably farmed.
- It's easiest to ask your fishmonger to scale the fish, but if you forget, then use the blunt edge of a large knife to scrape the scales off. Always rinse scales off sinks and surfaces with cold water: hot water glues them on!

STILTON

Most of us feel that stilton is an intrinsic part of Christmas, but
by the first weekend of the year mine is looking pockmarked
and unappetising. And the last thing I feel like is tucking into
an increasingly pongy bit of cheese and biscuits. Using it up
in cooking is the answer, but do be careful - too much can
overwhelm other flavours. Here are some ideas for dishes
that make the most of this powerful blue cheese.

POTTED STILTON
Serves 4
Preparation time: 20 minutes + 24 hours chilling

Simple and foolproof, potted stilton is a fantastic way of using up the last scraps. Eat it with Melba toast and ripe pears.

110 g (4 oz) leftover stilton
60 g (2 oz) butter, soft but not oily
1 dessertspoonful port

Crumble the soft parts of the stilton and grate any hard bits, discarding the rind. Mix with the butter and port (when I'm out of port I use crème de cassis – blackcurrant liqueur). Pot in a ramekin and leave in the fridge for 24 hours for the flavours to develop. Bring to room temperature before serving.

Rena Stanley, Buxton, Derbyshire

Leek, Potato and Stilton Soup
Serves 4–6
Preparation and cooking time: 1 hour

This is a soothing soup to beat the winter blues. As with all
recipes using stilton, the quantity needed will depend on how
mature and powerfully flavoured it is: nothing is worse than
a dish over-pungent with blue cheese. So trust your judgement
and feel free to use less (or more) than the amount suggested.

    450 g (1 lb) leeks, sliced and washed
    450 g (1 lb) floury potatoes, diced
    60 g (2 oz) butter
    1 litre (2 pints) hot vegetable or chicken stock
    approx 110 g (4 oz) stilton (not the hard rind)
    140 ml (5 fl oz) cream (optional)
    parsley, chopped

Cook the potatoes and leeks gently in the butter until the leeks
are softened. Add the hot stock and simmer for 35 minutes. Put
through a mouli-legumes (or purée in a food processor, although
the texture won't be quite as good). Return to the pan, but off
the heat, and add the crumbled stilton little by little, stirring until
it has melted in and tasting as you go. Stop adding the stilton
when the flavour is strong enough for you. Reheat gently, adding
cream if you like, and sprinkle over chopped parsley.

James Stark, Sheffield

TURKEY

I think I like turkey leftovers better than the hot roast, which is just as well since there always seems to be lots around. Do play safe with the cold bird though: store it in the fridge and use it up within 3 days. If that isn't possible, then strip the flesh from the bones on Boxing Day and make a stock with the carcass (see p.203). Any meat that isn't going to be eaten up imminently can then be bagged up and frozen for a month or so – although then I'd use it in cooked dishes, like the one that follows.

Mozzarella and Pine Nut Turkey

Serves 6
Preparation time: 25 minutes
Cooking time: 30 minutes

This tastes much less rich than it sounds, perhaps because the cooking apple adds a bit of acidity, like a squeeze of lemon or sour cream. Meanwhile, the cumin magically brings out the flavour of the meat. Don't be put off by the long list of ingredients: it's very easy to make.

   6-10 rashers streaky bacon, roughly chopped
   2 heaped tsp ground cumin
   2 leeks, washed and sliced
   1 onion, sliced
   a few cloves garlic, chopped
   280 ml (½ pint) single cream
   150 g (5 oz) mozzarella cheese, grated
   1 large cooking apple, peeled, cored, and grated
   150 g (5 oz) pine nuts
   2 glasses dry white wine
   500-750 g (1-1½ lb) cooked turkey, cut into chunks

Fry the bacon gently in a large frying pan for 3 or 4 minutes. Add the cumin, then the leeks, onion, and garlic, and continue cooking until the leeks and onion are softened. Meanwhile, heat the cream and slowly stir in the mozzarella to form a thick creamy mixture. Add the contents of the frying pan and the rest of the ingredients except the turkey, and stir together. Arrange the turkey in a buttered, ovenproof dish. Pour over the cream mixture and bake at Gas Mark 6/200°C/400°F for 30 minutes. Serve with rice and salad.

Graham Phillips, Hope Cove, Devon

CHRISTMAS "BRAWN"
Serves 6 as a starter
Preparation time: 30 minutes + 6 hours setting

A real brawn is made from pig's head and was once a traditional Christmas dish – but rest assured that this version has more conventional festive ingredients. This will make the purists tut, but I don't care. It might be my top turkey recipe of the season: a delicious, moist, and very low fat terrine, with chunks of meat suspended in a richly flavoured jelly. Perfect post-Christmas food, eat it with toast or salad.

   4 tbsp dry or medium dry sherry
   1 sachet powdered gelatine
   425 ml (15 fl oz) homemade turkey or chicken stock
   500 g (1 lb) cooked turkey, or turkey and ham, cut into
   1 cm (½ in) pieces
   1 tbsp tarragon chopped
   1 tbsp shelled pistachios, chopped

First, examine your stock: if it has set to a jelly in the fridge you can reduce the amount of gelatine by half or three-quarters. (Although the recipe calls for powdered gelatine, you could just as well use leaf gelatine, which is easier use and gives a crystal-clear result.) Put the sherry in a cup and sprinkle over the gelatine. Put to one side for a few minutes to allow it to swell. Heat the stock, remove from the heat, and add the gelatine, stirring until it is dissolved. Leave to cool out of the fridge for about 30 minutes. Choose your mould: either six ramekins or a loaf tin or plastic box holding 600 ml (1 pint). Pour in half the stock mixture and add half the meat, tarragon, and nuts. Refrigerate until it is just beginning to set, then add the rest of the ingredients. Put back in the fridge to set completely. Turn the brawn out by dipping the container briefly in hot water and inverting it on to a plate. This is good served with a mustard mayonnaise.

Andrea Leeman, Bristol

Turkey Pâté
Preparation time: 15 minutes + chilling time

This turkey pâté is a sort of meat paste, but in another class from those jars of beige spread that school sandwiches were made from. It's a great way of using up the very last vestiges of the festive meal, excellent on toast, and even better, as Mrs Rice suggests, in a sandwich with crispy bacon.

> leftover scraps of turkey
> leftover stuffing or sausagemeat (optional)
> butter
> turkey jelly
> salt
> freshly ground black pepper
> sherry or fresh herbs (optional)

Put all the scraps of turkey, excluding the skin, into a food processor (add the stuffing and/or sausagemeat if using). Melt a lump of butter (you want a turkey:butter ratio of about 4:1) with any jelly left from the turkey serving platter and underneath the turkey dripping. Add this mixture to the meat and whizz until smooth. Season with salt, pepper, and perhaps a splash of sherry, a few herbs, or what you will. Pack into a small dish and chill for at least 2 hours.

Karin Rice, Lymington, Hampshire

HOMEMADE POULTRY STOCK
Makes around 2.5 litres (4½ pints)
Preparation and cooking time: up to 12 hours

Even if you don't usually make your own stock, do it at
Christmas. Turkey bones make good stock, which in turn is
fantastic as a base for soups and risottos. If you have a slow
cooker (and I know many of you dust yours down to heat up
the Christmas pudding) then it's ideal – just chuck everything
in and leave it on overnight. But even made the conventional
way, it's not difficult, and the results will transform your cooking.
Stock freezes well, but you may want to boil it down to make
a concentrate first, so it doesn't take up too much space.

> 1 turkey (or chicken or goose) carcass
> giblets
> 1 onion, studded with two cloves
> 1 carrot
> 1 stick of celery
> 6–8 peppercorns
> 1 bay leaf

Put the carcass and giblets (but not the liver), together with
any jellied juices, into your biggest pan. Add the rest of the
ingredients. Cover with water, then simmer gently (boiled stock
is cloudy) all day, spooning off any white scum that floats to
the surface. Strain the stock through a fine sieve, cool, and
refrigerate. Lift off any fat floating on the top (it should have
solidified) and discard.

Xanthe Clay

INDEX